TAKING IT TO THE MAX

An Autobiography

MAXIE HAYLES

To Christine Gaishard
With Compliments,
"Intellegence is a prouiledge
not a right, so you
should use it wizely"
October 35th 2016
M. A. Hayles

HANSIB

First Published in 2016 by Hansib Publications Limited
P. O. Box 226, Hertford, SG14 3WY
United Kingdom

info@ hansibpublications.com
www.hansibpublications.com

ISBN 978-1-910553-68-8

A CIP catalogue record for this book
is available from the British Library

Produced by Hansib Publications

Printed in Great Britain

The Author

Jamaican born Maxie Hayles has lived in England for over 56 years and during that time has led a well fought campaign alongside others as a community and human rights activist. In his memoirs entitled *Taking It To The Max* he uses his own style, approach and words to bring to the reader a lot of what it feels like to experience almost every perceivable struggle and strife as a black man fighting the pernicious evil racism. His life has not been easy and to use a Jamaican saying 'Who feels it knows it.' His selfless approach on the 'frontline' championing and challenging just causes for the betterment of society is highly respected, admired and commended having contributed vastly in helping to make Britain and the world a better place.

Life for Maxie Hayles began in Pennington, St. Catherine, rural Jamaica with a deep rooted sense of family values in a Christian belief system. On arriving in Britain as a teenager in 1960 was for him a major cultural shock. This autobiography with many highs and lows on that journey of life makes compelling reading and is in every sense of the word what can be described as a page turner. It is filled with sadness, humour, pain, laughter, anger and joy in the numerous adventures, trials, tribulations and conflicts as he endeavoured to take it to another level sometimes against all the odds. Among his accolades and achievements was being named the winner of the 2000 Prime Minister's Regional and National Active Community Award for building a fair and just community which clearly shows the pinnacle of his success.

Maxie the older of his mother Doris Amanda Lewis's two children had a loving and close relationship with her until she departed this world on the 9th December 2014, three weeks short of her 90th birthday. Her death had a major impact on him and he made the decision to dedicate his autobiography to her memory. The married father of two has shown how with determination one can triumph in the face of adversity.

Maxie strongly felt the need to document for posterity an account of his journey. So this is his story or put another way, this is his history, for others to read, digest and hopefully get something positive from. A truly revealing, inspirational and open testament of Maxie's life.

Doris Amanda Lewis, Maxie Hayles's mother in her heyday.

Dedication

I dedicate this book to my dear beloved mother Mrs. Doris Amanda Lewis who was born on the 9th January 1925 and departed this life on the 9th December 2014. It goes without saying that had it not been for her unconditional love along with her firm but fair approach in terms of her parenting skills, I would not have accomplished most of what I had set out to do in my life.

My mother will always remain close to my heart and in my thoughts. May she rest in eternal peace and rise in glory when hopefully we will meet again in God's Kingdom.

Contents

Acknowledgements

There are a number of individuals whom I need to express my heartfelt gratitude, thanks and appreciation for all that they have done to make this autobiography a living reality. Without them I would not have been able to succeed with this book writing project and it hammers home the well known saying that 'No man is an island, no man stands alone' as this was truly an altruistic effort involving others whom I must now mention and give due credit.

First and foremost I thank Jesus Christ the Living Lord for giving me the health, strength, wisdom and understanding along with faith and endurance to achieve this goal of writing my memoirs. I firmly believe that all things are possible if you put your trust in God and He has helped me to accomplish this project.

I would like to thank my immediate family, my wife, daughter, son and son-in-law for all the love and support that they have given to me throughout this labour of love. Their unstinting and unwavering loyalty has encouraged me every step of the way and I am truly grateful.

Dr. Martin Glynn, writer, criminologist, lecturer at Birmingham City University was very instrumental in giving me guidance and direction in the initial stages on how to structure my memoirs and I thank him wholeheartedly for all that he has done in that regard. Additional thanks are due to him for his input in helping to edit, proof read and write the foreword.

My good friend of many years Tony Kelly has worked assiduously on this project spending a lot of his time, effort and energy with me including doing all of the typing. He has helped to proof read and edit the manuscript whilst offering valuable advice and guidance throughout the project in order to make this autobiography become a reality. For his invaluable contribution and diligence I am eternally grateful. The hospitality afforded to me by his wife Rose and their daughter Abigail at their home over a lengthy period of time during the writing of my memoirs deserves recognition and appreciation and I sincerely thank them from the bottom of my heart.

Shirley Finch the administrator of the Afro Caribbean Millennium Centre (ACMC) in Birmingham has been a tower of strength in every way possible and I cannot thank her enough for all that she has done in enabling this book to come to fruition.

Finally, I would like to place on record my sincere thanks to Bishop Wilton Powell, Gordon Weaver, Gillian McPherson, Andy Hamilton, Doreen Osborne, Georgina Mendez, Audrey Adams, Simon Woolley, Lee Jasper, Shane Ward, Phillip Murphy, Pastor Bryan Scott, Pastor Clifford Fryer, Terry Brathwaite, Ashok Viswanathan, Errol Robinson, Carl Morgan and Operation Black Vote (OBV) for all their support and encouragement in the writing of my memoirs.

Foreword

The socio-cultural function of an 'autobiography' is for an individual to present an account of their life based on thoughtful reflection regarding significant events in their lives. The outcome then forms the basis of a selective 'personal narrative' where the reader will be able to gain important insights into the life of the author. The importance here is that an autobiography becomes an important document rooted within a 'social history' context. All too often within marginalised (black) communities the personalised stories and wider community narrative is at the mercy of a biased media, subject to a lack of resourcing, or at worst absent from the wider community history. It is also true that at times important personal contributions to the communities' social life are badly negated, hardly ever promoted, or even validated. For this reason Maxie's story becomes less of 'a community eulogy' but more of an important contribution of 'community history' presented by someone who has not only lived a colourful life, but had a significant impact within the various communities and spaces he has lived and worked in.

Brazilian Augusto Boal was in sympathy with oppressed people and believed in humanity's ability to change. Boal developed 'Theatre of the Oppressed', a form of participatory theatre that uses cooperative forms of interaction amongst marginalised and disaffected groups. His revolutionary democratic approach to theatre is an important tool used to fight oppression in the daily lives of those at the margins of society.

Similarly, Maxie's account of his life has been designed as an important 'legacy' designed to assist the next generation in learning about a past that has been rendered invisible. Maxie's telling of his life reveals some raw truths, challenges and contests some of the myths surrounding the nature of the contemporary 'Black Experience' as well as giving an insight into the person himself; father, brother, husband etc. The contrast between Maxie's personal and professional selves reveals him to be a complex, vulnerable, challenging, and more importantly a committed individual, who believes in the pursuit of justice, regardless of whether he is the beneficiary of any outcomes.

Maxie's desire for justice started in his childhood and has been a consistent feature throughout his life. Eminent qualitative research advocate Norman Denzin argues that for 'subordinated voices' to be heard, they must be 'helped to speak'. Equally as important is the view of another important communications scholar Arthur Bochner, who writes in his book *Coming to Narrative* where he states:

> Listening to different voices and trying to express your own, about trying to muster the courage to speak the unspoken even if it terrifies you, (p 315).

Both Denzin and Bochner highlight the need for all of us to reveal our 'own truths' and to tell our own stories if we are to transcend the limitations imposed on us, or in turn what we impose on ourselves. Maxie's story reveals the importance of confronting ourselves, addressing the issues that come to the surface, and being vulnerable enough to place it in the public domain. In a free society the telling of 'your truth' is not an offense, illegal, nor should it be subject to censorship. Indeed Maxie's recounting of his experiences will no doubt resonate with those who feel that he may have distorted the truth, or feels that his account of things are biased. To those people I would urge you to consider taking a non-judgemental stance. Telling your truth in an open and honest way can sometimes be 'raw', 'bitter' and even 'upsetting'. However, Maxie has provided many other sides to his story that are tinged with humour, positive experiences, and some very touching moments. For many people who know Maxie, this autobiographical account of his life will reveal many other layers of his personality that will enable his friends and critics alike to understand those circumstances that have shaped this extraordinary character. From his early days in Jamaica, his formative years in the UK, the struggles to establish himself professionally, contrast with his continuous journey to establish himself as a father, husband and a member of a church and professional organisations.

What is clearly evident is Maxie is someone who has stood for something, argued for the right to exist as a human being and has refused to accept any form of subordination. In the telling of his story Maxie has also expressed regrets, been self-critical, as well as openly criticising publicly things he has felt were wrong. In doing so, Maxie is following a tradition of personal narratives, which have emerged from all facets of history related to displaced men and women. Most of all Maxie's story is an important 'legacy project' designed to give an insight into one person's experiences, engagement with, and connection to, a time and space which is seldom documented. In doing so Maxie has provided us with a template for discussion in barber shops, churches, colleges and universities, community spaces and so on. In doing so *Taking it to the Max* is a welcome addition to a community that at times fears expressing itself for fear of not being heard.

Dr. Martin Glynn: writer, criminologist and lecturer at City of Birmingham University

Introduction

'A people without the knowledge of their past history, origin and culture is like a tree without roots.'
—Marcus Mosiah Garvey(17/8/1887–10/6/1940). Jamaica National Hero

I Maxie Alphonso Hayles decided that I had reached a stage in my life where sharing with others my life experiences, my journey, my trials, my tribulations, my battles as well as my hopes and fears was imperative so that they can fully understand and appreciate the proverb, 'From little acorns oak trees grow'. I am therefore going to take you all on this journey mapping out my humble beginnings in rural Jamaica to life in England, where I came to reside at a young age. I can assure you that it was never a bed of roses or an easy life, as unlike some others I was not born with a silver spoon in my mouth nor had a silver platter on my lap. It has always been about ambition, drive, passion, hard work, faith and determination to get to where I am, helping those less fortunate along the way whilst trying my utmost to show selfless concern for the well-being of others. Therefore, self sacrifices and self-denial along my university of life have been many and I remain eternally indebted, grateful and thankful to my dear wife, our two children as well as in more recent times my son-in-law for all the support, love and understanding that they have given to me.

This autobiography is living proof that I am more than ready, willing and able to write, share and present my experiences and adventures with no one questioning that I have not lived long enough in order to document for future generations my life story. Unlike some autobiographies written in other people's tender years, my approach is based on the well known Jamaican phrase *'Young bud nuh know hurricane'* meaning young people have not yet lived or experienced life long enough to be penning their life story. Put another way, some are still babies in nappies in the grand scheme of things and it is therefore not surprising that by the time some are in their mid forties they have already attempted to write their third autobiography.

In writing my memoirs it has proven to be a roller coaster of a journey filled with emotions of happiness, joy, sadness, anger, grief, heartache and pain. To reminisce and resurrect aspects of my life which just like every human being may have both negative and positive factors, is therapeutic in many ways and similar to cleansing ones soul. I am pleased to have finally committed my life story to print not just as a personal account but from a sociological, empirical, spiritual and historical perspective of my trials, struggles and tribulations as a black man.

In the black community there is an established tradition of oral history being passed down the generations and not being documented for posterity for others to read, digest and act accordingly. In embarking on this project, my intention has been fulfilled in that I am in the fortunate position to be one of those persons who will be able to leave behind in print and in the public domain a detailed account of who Maxie Hayles really is and why *Taking It To The Max* is the chosen title. What I am sharing with you in this autobiography is first hand information and knowledge, as no one knows their own life story better than the individual concerned. It is after all my lived experience and my reality which no one can deny me of.

It has not been easy getting this project of my life story off the ground. And it is fair to say some people who I had asked to come on board over time, have ended up disappointing me in not keeping their promises and not being able to deliver. But then again in thinking positively nothing happens before the time and looking back on it the time was not right. With God's grace and help, as I put my trust in Him, along with my determination and will power to succeed quite similar to what I have experienced in life this book is a living testament of the struggles and upheavals that I have encountered along the way and how I have overcome them. Thus the moral of this story is to never give up and to keep pursuing your dreams and aspirations as you will succeed in the end. Put another way, Napoleon Hill's proverbial saying *'A quitter never wins and a winner never quits'* resonates with me in a huge way.

There have been a lot of highs and lows, triumphs and setbacks which are all a part of life. At times in the past I have found myself wondering why certain things have happened to me or what have I done to deserve them but with my Christian faith I always leave it in the hands of God. We all can look back and ponder what if? Or contemplate whether one should have gone down a different path at various crossroads in life. However as much as one wants to look back one must endeavour to look forward and by so doing move on with a positive mental attitude. That in my view is the best approach whilst on life's major learning curve. The words of the song 'Que-sera-sera, whatever will be will be' sung by the late Doris Day perfectly sum up for me one's fate, one's destiny, changing the course of one's life and history, as that is my lived and real experience.

Throughout this book one will notice a biblical quote at the beginning of each chapter as that reaffirms my faith in God and at the end of each chapter due to my cultural heritage and background I have included a Jamaican proverb along with the translation.

I hope you find this journey of mine inspiring, uplifting, thought provoking and educational. If there is only one thing positive that you as the reader get from this historical account of my life story, it would have been worthwhile sharing with you the many and varied adventures.

Chapter 1
Mum and I

*'For I know the plans I have for you' declares the Lord,
'plans to prosper you and not to harm you, plans to give you
hope and a future.'*
—Jeremiah 29 verse 11.

I intend to focus on the early years of my childhood in Jamaica including her role as a disciplinarian, an educator, a mother and a friend. I was born in 1943 in the district of Pennington in the parish of St. Catherine, the first child of my mother Doris Amanda Mills who was affectionately called 'Coolie Gal' because of her light skinned complexion and her long flowing hair. My father George Hayles (born 1919, died 13th April 1996) originated from the district of Cudjoe's Hill in the same parish. As his first son I was born out of wedlock. The fact that my parents were not married to each other is totally irrelevant even though society at the time frowned on people in a similar situation not being the product of a married union. Thankfully, times have changed and as a result society has become more non-judgemental, more accommodating and more understanding on that issue.

My father worked at the famous Innswood Sugar estate near Spanish Town prior to his departure to England. Following the death of his beloved wife he decided without much thought and having spent so many years in England to return to the land of his birth. He made the all important decision to do so after only one visit home in the many years that he had resided in this country. That single visit seemed to convince him of his desire to return there permanently and there was no stopping him. My father built a house on land in Old Road district in St. Catherine that he had purchased before coming to England. He lived in his home for a number of years along with one of his daughters, Miss D and her children. My wife and I visited him on a number of occasions whilst on trips home to the beautiful island and it was a pleasure to see him so relaxed and at peace being far away from the maddening crowd. After his death the decision was made by the five remaining siblings to bring back his body to England to be buried in a twin grave with his wife who had predeceased him. I was really upset by my father's death and he is forever in my thoughts as I loved him dearly. I was not fortunate enough to have met my grandfather Henry Hayles on my father's side as a child because he died before I was born. However I met his wife who is my grandmother named Therza Thomas affectionately known as Sis and visited her regularly at her home in Cudjoe's Hill.

It is very sad each time I remember how my mother such a loving, kind and family oriented person, was never shown that love and affection by her own father James Mills during her life, as he practically ignored her for a great deal of the time. She was not the product of his marriage and he seemed to have taken the attitude which is deeply worrying of some men who father children and then accept no responsibility for helping to raise or financially support them. He did not disown her but chose not to acknowledge her publicly. It took the efforts of his other children to eventually in later life bridge the gap and try to mend the almost non-existent relationship. She was finally accepted by the entire family after she came to England and was able to be reunited with the same Jamaican siblings, some of whom were now living here. My mother was the spitting image of all the Mills family and the resemblance was so real that the phrase 'Chip nuh fly far from de block' would be an accurate description. Unlike now when DNA is often asked for as evidence or proof of paternity, it was certainly not needed in this case. As a consequence of this I have never had a relationship with my grandfather and that saddens me because I too always felt like an outsider in the same way my mother did.

During that era the Jamaican tradition and heritage put a great deal of emphasis on the first born male child. Since I fitted the mould there were a lot of expectations placed on my shoulders and it was incumbent upon me to step up to the mark and deliver accordingly. That mindset is similar to the position of British royalty where the heir to the throne until fairly recently with a change in the law in Parliament had to be male. This outdated issue of male heirs was finally discredited and abandoned, due to it being both sexist and discriminatory towards women, as well as having no place or relevance in modern day society.

My younger sister was born three years later and we three lived with the extended family of my great grandmother affectionately called 'Mumma', on my mother's side. Her name was Annie Johnson Prince. This is a tradition well established for centuries in African communities where the village takes care of raising the children. Hence the Igbo and Yoruba (Nigerian) proverb, 'It takes a whole village to raise a child' best sums up my early childhood upbringing. Also in the district was my grandmother Florence Henry who was the mother of my mother.

The area that I was raised in Pennington is literally called Plantation, which is reminiscent of slavery plantations with several acres of land and the slave owner being in charge of his stock. Luckily for us that was not the situation as slavery had been abolished in the British empire on 1st August 1834. Later I will mention the impact this had on my great grandmother 'Mumma' having been born in the 1800's.

This period of my childhood with no electricity or piped water, meant we had to fetch water from a stream down a steep gully at an area we nicknamed Brukway, (Broke Away). The name was derived because the soil erosion meant each time we attempted to head there we would if not careful lose our footing/grip and tumble down the steep hill. This water meant for domestic use was being carried on our head in containers as we returned from the treacherous ravine via Sam Hill which was also another steep incline. That was a picture of rural Jamaica back in the late forties and fifties but one which I really enjoyed. Sometimes by the time we arrived home a lot of the water had spilled out of the containers and our clothes were soaked.

I recall vividly a man in our district named Mr. Clarence repeatedly telling me stories of his experience in the 2nd World War (1939–1945). Being a soldier in the British army he was stationed in Belgium, as Jamaica played its part under the colonial rule of the British Empire. *Lest we forget* which is a direct reference to Rudyard Kipling's 1897 poem *Recessional* used in Remembrance Day ceremonies as a caution against forgetting those who died in war, a large contingent of black soldiers from the West Indies fought alongside British armed forces during that war and the 1st World War. So those tales of his adventures still resonate with me, as he remembered how with other soldiers he marched in Belgium and spoke about it with a sense of excitement and pride. As a little boy I was intrigued by his stories of war which have stuck in my memory, even though I now realise and acknowledge that wars should be avoided at all cost in favour of diplomatic solutions. However I also accept that tyranny, genocide and other forms of brutality inflicted on innocent people have to be defeated by force when appropriate.

Before beginning my primary school education I attended a private school run by Miss Lowther Gordon. Such a school in Jamaica is usually referred to as 'basic school' and she started me on my educational journey of learning to read and write. She was the first person to put a pencil in my hand therefore teaching me how to write.

There was a little boy named Winston Hayles whose pet name was Ken and being two brother's children we were first cousins. The family connection was even closer as my mother in whose memory this book is dedicated was closely related to Ken's mother. My happiest childhood memories were shared with Ken doing all the wonderful things children enjoy at that age. Sadly he will not be able to see in print how much I remember our good times together as children as he passed away in 2014 in Jamaica after returning from the United States of America where he had lived for many years. Ken and I used to kill lizards, bury them in green banana leaves and sang over their dead bodies as if it was a funeral, although we were in our naivety being cruel to God's creatures.

Ken was left handed. He had what in boxing terms would be referred to as a 'South Paw', which made him one of the best kneaders of the dough used in making fried dumplings, commonly known as 'Johnny Cakes' and boiled dumplings. We shared everything as youngsters. He was one of the best drivers on some of Jamaica's rocky and winding roads whilst he in later life worked for Hannah Town Bakery (HTB) delivering bread and bun to shops and supermarkets. We, along with others enjoyed playing one of Jamaica's favourite sports cricket, with bats made out of coconut bough with limes or oranges as the cricket ball on a piece of level land at Plantation.

In rural Jamaica during the mango season (June-August) which coincided with the school summer holidays, the mangoes would fall from the trees mainly overnight so Ken and I took great delight in the early morning before the others awoke, to go and find these sweet and delicious fruits. There was a stream running close to where we lived and we also went there to find avocado pears as well as attempting to catch small fishes, crayfish and shrimps hiding under the rocks. We also made slingshots and killed birds which were roasted on an open fire. We created our own entertainment with the limb from the coconut tree, riding on it down a steep hill shrieking with laughter and excitement. Modern day theme parks pale in comparison when I look back on those fun filled days of my childhood, with the only technology for these exhilarating rides being the coconut bunker and the hill to which we would race back to the top to repeat the daring ride several times. It certainly kept us active, fit and was so enjoyable.

Some of the Jamaican meals that I relished as a child were cornmeal porridge, cornmeal dumpling, Irish Moss and Linseed, 'Mackerel Run Dung' with coconut milk and susumba also known as gully beans even though they had a bitter taste. Alongside those dishes was an abundance of fresh fruits such as ripe bananas, guineps, star apples, jackfruits, mangoes, sour sops, papayas, tamarind and sugar cane to mention a few.

My mother was a brilliant cook and her mouth watering dishes, especially the baked products would put most Michelin starred chefs to shame. She used to make 'Duckunoo' or 'Blue Drawers' with grated sweet potato sometimes referred to as 'Tie-a-leaf' because it was wrapped in a green banana leaf and then boiled. She knew that I really loved it. As far as I am concerned nobody makes that treat better than the ones she prepared for me as they were truly scrumptious. Oh the joys of my childhood which I would relive anytime soon as they were filled with such happy and pleasant memories. And to think that laptop computers, mobile phones, tablets, video games consoles and the internet were not even thought of, let alone existed in those days in Jamaica.

It is important to make reference to the fact that during my early upbringing I was always surrounded by black people and my closest connections with any white persons were my godparents Mr. and Mrs. Batchelor. They were of a fair skinned complexion which was as close to white as one could ever imagine. The poem *Pass Fi White* by the late Dr. Louise Bennett one of Jamaica's outstanding poets of Patois, a comedienne, story teller and icon of Jamaican folklore, readily comes to mind. Jamaican Patois known locally as (Patwa or Patwah) and called Jamaican Creole by linguists is an English-based creole language with West African influences (a majority of loan words of Akan origin) spoken primarily in Jamaica and the Jamaican Diaspora.

Two verses of *Pass Fi White* by Louise Bennett:

Miss Jane jus hear from Merica
Her daughter proudly write
Fi seh she fail her exam, but
She passin dere fi white!

She seh fi tell de trute she know
Her brain part not so bright –
She couldn pass tru college
So she try fi pass fi white.

There were only a few televisions whilst I was growing up in Jamaica in the fifties and they constantly showed images of white people. That in itself has always been a bone of contention in the Jamaican society for many decades as the few white people living there were held in higher esteem over the black majority population as a result of such mental enslavement. They had inherited land, wealth, positions of status and power and constantly kept black people in subservient roles. The motto of Jamaica based on its 6th August 1962 Independence declaration from colonial Britain is 'Out of Many, One People' and over time there has been a shift in that regard. But there is still a long way to go towards parity and equity as 'the haves and the have-nots' remain a controversial issue and Jamaica still has several examples of social class prejudice.

I attended Juan de Bolas Primary School in the same district and later Point Hill (Bottom) School some distance away. After awhile I was forced to leave the first school mentioned because whilst playing a game of 'Cowboys and Indians' as little boys did in those days I had a small pen knife which I used in all innocence to injure one of the other children. With the benefit of hindsight my action of injuring that child was mirroring how the Native American Indians were portrayed in films and comic books and I had taken make belief and turned it in to reality, a mistake for which I suffered the consequences. This caused a lot of bother and tension in the district and my mother therefore thought it was in my best interest to attend Point Hill (Bottom) School. Having to suddenly be sent to another school really affected me as a child since I was known for being quiet, well behaved and well mannered and was totally devastated by the turn of events. As an elder I now actively encourage the younger generation to avoid the knife culture that is impacting on their lives and emphasise to them the danger of carrying one as part of their possessions. It is after all an offensive weapon and ultimately can lead to death. Even now in our household I insist that all the knives in the kitchen are faced downward, as with the sharp pointed edge it can be a dangerous weapon if one accidentally brushes against it.

I distinctly remember having to cross Pompey river every day to and from Point Hill Primary school, jumping or walking over stones so as not to get wet, which is something most children who all love water would probably do. One day in particular it rained heavily and this was my only route to get home. I still chanced crossing and bearing in mind that I was never taught to swim I did not realise the depth of the current of water that was flowing downstream from the torrential rain that had fallen. As I was on my own at the time I tried desperately to get to the other side against the strong current and could have drowned. This is an experience that I will never forget as it is embedded in my memory bank. I am sure one of my nine lives as the proverbial saying goes in reference to cats, left me that day. I vaguely remember seeing a male figure as an apparition which I think might have been my guardian angel. The power of the Almighty God guided me through that traumatic experience and I am truly thankful to be alive in order to share it with you.

After that terrible and frightening event which I related to my mother, she out of concern for my safety, welfare and sensing the danger I was put through, moved me to Point Hill district to live with my aunt Ciscelyn who lived across the road from the school where I remained a pupil. My mother as the sole bread winner was now residing in the capital city Kingston, earning a living to support my sister and I whilst relying on extended family members for their hands-on approach in looking after us in rural Jamaica.

A vivid memory of my early childhood as an eight year old in Pennington, Jamaica was the 1951 storm known as hurricane

Charlie. There was a lot of talk about it with strong winds and my pet animal a chicken (fowl) called 'Mother Hen', given to me by my formidable great grandmother 'Mumma', was laying eggs at that time. So can you just imagine my excitement at the possibility of experiencing my first ever hurricane? My beloved hen sheltered in a coop behind the house and survived the terrible storm and if she could talk would tell the tale of how she managed to do so. I supposed I got the spirit to fight throughout my life and adopt survival instincts from seeing my pet hen struggle through the strong winds to come through the storm unscathed.

My mother showed her tender loving care towards both of her children and always gave sound and firm motherly advice as we grew up. She was a strict disciplinarian and by her actions one of her abiding principles was not sparing the rod and spoiling the child. So apart from getting my fair share of beatings whenever like most children I stepped out of line, later in life she spoke about a television news report of a young girl caught shoplifting. My mother was so incensed and said that she needed a good 'hiding'. I explained to her that could be viewed as cruelty adding that she could end up being arrested. With her sense of humour, her dead pan response was along the lines of she would beat the police and if taken to court would also beat the judge. She said it in jest but in a way meant every word. This showed her passion for discipline as she certainly did not suffer fools gladly no matter what their position or status was in society or indeed the circumstances. However do not misunderstand her stance as she was indeed a law abiding person with strong Christian beliefs and principles.

My great grandmother, 'Mumma' was the first person who made me aware of the word 'Backra' which was the name given to the white plantation owner of the period even after slavery came to an end. She was born in the 1800's and lived, experienced and knew what the remnants of slavery were all about. Growing up as a child meant hearing stories from her about having to work on the Worthy Park sugar estate in St Catherine and of the most unpleasant and hard working conditions that she had to endure under the supervision of the 'Backra' or Master.

Mumma's husband Mr. Prince thought that I had a good singing voice and taught me the words of a song which in part were "Please take me back to Ethiopia, let me go mark out my burial spot, it is a land of liberty where corn and wine is awaiting me, it is no wonder my heart is fond of Ethiopia". I used to have to sing it back to him and still remember the words. That resonates with me in a big way and little did he know all those many years ago that he was actually preparing me for the life of championing equality and justice. So this clearly demonstrates the conscious, vibrant, political and powerful lyrics blowing in the air over sixty years ago which make the talk nowadays of this desire for wanting to return to the homeland Africa seem a new concept, even though it has been around for a very long time.

As stated earlier, I did not grow up with my father who was a pre-trained teacher. He was blind in one eye from glaucoma and was unable to fulfil his true potential in terms of furthering his education due to financial constraints and ill health. However I saw him on a regular basis during my childhood whilst visiting his family home in Red Hills, St. Catherine near to Guanaboa Vale. On many of those journeys to visit him which was quite a few miles from where I was living, I relied heavily on the kindness of a man affectionately known as 'Sweet Foot'. He got that nickname because of his driving style, revving the accelerator and clutch of a van in such a way that it was exciting to witness and listen to from the sounds it made as a delivery driver of freshly baked hard dough bread, buns and bulla cakes for Sunbeam Bakery to various shops. I was eternally grateful for those lifts as on the odd occasion I had to commute the distance on foot in the hot scorching sun which was rather unpleasant.

As a child one does not really get bogged down with petty jealousy so I did not view any of the children he had with his wife with scepticism and used to look forward to meeting and playing with them. My father also had two other children from another relationship, namely Miss D, and Clarice who is now deceased.

Due to my father's educational capabilities, in later years he was often consulted as the fountain of knowledge by the extended family, being best able to give a wealth of advice on a range of financial matters. He truly had a wise head on his body and family members would always seek out his counsel and guidance when needed. Some family members are now not surprised at how I have become a point of reference on various issues as well.

I recall with a great deal of accuracy witnessing domestic abuse and being subjected to child abuse as Ernest, my mother's partner at the time, physically assaulted her in the family home. Although I was small in stature as a child I stood up to that bully but did not realise that his actions were considered to be domestic abuse. By standing up for my mother which was the most natural thing to do, to my shock and horror he threw a bucket of cold water over me later on whilst I was lying in bed. This has stuck in my memory as if it were yesterday. In addition to that, he arranged for one of his nephews who was twice my size considering I was only ten years old to beat me up, which he did. I despise anyone who bullies another person and uses their strength and size to harm a child or someone who is vulnerable. Thankfully my mother especially with the help of my grand uncle Leonard Morrison affectionately called Uncle Lenny ended that relationship despite Ernest's repeated threats and intimidation.

On one occasion even after the relationship ended the abusive Ernest continued to harass, intimidate and threaten my mother and, I ended up running nearly ten miles to Pennington to fetch Uncle Lenny who was known as the protector of the family. We arrived back at Point Hill and he armed with a machete which he sharpened with his file throughout the journey as it glistened in the hot sun made contact with Ernest. A crowd of onlookers gathered to see what was going to happen and Uncle Lenny dared Ernest to touch my mother again as by this time he had assembled others of his family members and friends to support him. Each time I remember this incident in my life I think of the movie *High Noon* which had a similar scene played out in it, except that mine was real, not fiction and thus true to life. Ernest certainly met his match as my uncle rightly confronted him having developed a reputation of not standing for any nonsense especially in relation to his family and more so to my mother who was his favourite niece, always calling her 'Coolie Gal'. Ernest got his 'comeuppance' and with his supporters backed down from his threats towards my mother. Since then we have never been threatened by him and his band of followers. Later to the utter disbelief and shock of the family, Ernest attempted on his arrival in England to rekindle the relationship with my mother who told him where to 'get lost' in no uncertain terms.

I was also being bullied at school by another student and my class teacher was aware of this. I ended up fighting the bully in what was my first fight giving him a bloody nose and after that he never troubled me again. Standing up to bullies in every way, shape and form rubbed off on me from that tender age, which is why I have even to this day continued to fight institutional racism and individual racism along with all other forms of oppression which amount to bullying. Fighting the system, fighting injustice, fighting inequality, fighting discrimination and thus taking it to the max for others who are less able to do so have always been part of my nature. I still take a stand for those who are constantly trod on, marginalised and treated less favourably. The boy who bullied me had one of his cousins on the teaching staff and she in turn took it upon herself to harass me outside of school. However I soon 'fixed her business' by confronting her away from the school premises and she too stopped mistreating me. It suddenly dawned on me how brave my inner being was in confronting these bullies.

I was deemed to be one of the brightest students at school and was constantly praised by the teaching staff for the good work that I produced on a regular basis. Aunt Ciscelyn had to move elsewhere so I was sent to live close by with another caring woman who was not a relative but treated me like her own son. I do not know what was the cause but for some unknown reason I could not eat from her and it was nothing to do with hygiene or being unclean. My abiding memory was of her being heavily pregnant and I am left wondering whether that played on my mind causing me to withdraw from eating anything that she prepared. This meant that I could not stay there for long as I would have ended up starving so went to live in Kingston with my mother on Spanish Town Road before moving to Cockburn Pen.

Later my sister joined us in Kingston and I continued my education at Denham Town All Age school with believe it or not, my mother's favourite teacher Mr. Hawthorne who taught her at Point Hill Primary school. He was the headmaster of the school. My mother was simply overjoyed when she realised that was going to be the case. So the education and discipline that teacher Hawthorne had instilled in my mother was being passed on via his teaching methods to me. One could not write a better script than that as I was certainly in a conducive learning environment.

My love of chickens and eggs produced naturally continued when I resided in Kingston as my mother had some hens in the yard on Spanish Town Road which laid eggs, sold by her to buy my seaman khaki school uniform. This showed her ability to be self reliant as she made sure to provide for my sister and I.

At one point my mother had a relationship with Mr. Dyas my stepfather who was the watchman/caretaker at Desnoes and Geddes, (popularly known as D and G) the drinks factory of soda and Red Stripe beer on Spanish Town Road, Four Miles in Kingston. We lived on the premises as accommodation on site was a requirement of his job. In the mornings so that I could catch the bus to attend school in Denham Town my mother as fit as a fiddle would take me from our home to Three miles roundabout on her bicycle. I enjoyed the ride sitting on the tow bar and it was such a lovely feeling being taken on part of my journey to school by my mother. Bicycles were the rage in Jamaica at that time and with less vehicular traffic on the roads back in the late fifties meant pollution was never an issue and the air was fresh and clean.

The journey to school continued on a Jamaica Omnibus Service (JOS) bus and one of the regular drivers on that bus route was a man named George Powell who treated me like his son. He often made sure that I had pocket money and invited me to visit the bus depot in downtown Kingston not far from my school on a Friday morning after he was paid to buy me cakes and soda drinks. His generosity and kind spirit were really touching gestures and when he knew of my plans to migrate, my intention was to keep in touch with him and reciprocate the kindness that he offered to me. Unfortunately I lost contact with him and only later discovered by reading an article in a newspaper that he had died in what I believe were unfortunate circumstances. That was rather sad as I would have loved to have been there for him considering all he did for me as a youngster growing up. He really was a true and good human being in my eyes.

My stepfather Mr. Dyas got a new job in Flankers near Montego Bay the second city and initially he was on his own until we joined him sometime later. In the meantime my mother used to regularly give me goods and supplies to take from our home in Kingston on the train to Montego Bay. That is why I can still vividly remember even though I was only aged 14, the September 1st 1957 Kendal train crash in the parish of Manchester which killed 175 passengers and injured over 800. It was the second worst rail disaster in the world at that time and still remains the worst transport accident in Jamaica's history.

After that major train disaster I along with many other people from Kingston and the surrounding areas who were curious to know what had happened and wanted to see firsthand the survivors and witnesses, went along to the railway station terminus at Hunts Bay near to Four Miles where they were ferried to on another train. This tragedy has stayed with me all of those years and I often think what could have happened had I been on that train as one of the passengers since it was my custom at the time to visit my stepfather in Montego Bay.

Later in that same year 1957 my mother, sister and I as a family unit joined my stepfather in Flankers. I attended Montego Bay Boys School whilst my sister went to the girl's school next door. Interestingly whilst my sister and I were attending those schools, the school inspectors visited and lo and behold it was Mr. and Mrs. Hawthorne who had featured significantly in my education thus far. It was such a joy to see them yet again as he was one of my favourite teachers at Denham Town All Age School. He clearly left an indelible mark and impact on my early upbringing.

The journey from Flankers to the school was quite a distance and I walked barefoot to and from school. On several occasions as I made that journey there was a Syrian family who lived in the posh area of the city and never drove by if they noticed me walking to or from school. The mother who was always the driver would stop and offer me a lift which I gladly accepted. Such kindness has stayed in my memory bank all these years. I had fond memories of the route to school as the hotels got rid of the rubbish such as melon seeds which would as Mother Nature intended start to grow by the wayside thus producing fruits. This meant there was always an abundance of melons along the way which is probably why I have an abiding love for melons to this day.

Apart from the Syrian family another well dressed black man would see me walking and stop to offer me a lift bearing in mind in those days transportation was not as frequent as it is today and not forgetting the hot conditions even though it was early in the morning. Sadly on one occasion I somehow forgot to say 'Good morning' on entering his car and he without hesitation instructed me to get out. I was so shocked and bewildered as all he said was 'get out and learn manners'. It is something that I will never forget and knowing how I was brought up to display manners and respect for everyone, until now I am still unsure as to what I had done wrong. I was taught to always address people especially my elders with a salutation when meeting them and perhaps I slipped up badly on that one occasion as he never again offered me a lift which I found to be harsh.

The very first time that I ever earned money was as a part-time trainee during the extension of the Montego Bay Airport runway now known as Donald Sangster International Airport. Under supervision I was taught to drive the tractor/grader laying the foundation for the runway by the Chinese owner who took a liking to me. The money earned was especially helpful to the family as my stepfather who had been the breadwinner was terminally ill with cancer and unable to work. However there was a lot of petty jealousy on the part of other workers when I was taken on as a trainee tractor driver and to this day I struggle to understand their mentality as to why they resented the opportunity that I as a 15 year old was being given in order to earn a livelihood. Sadly my stepfather died whilst we were living in Montego Bay so we eventually came back to Kingston to reside in Maverley and I returned to Denham Town All Age School for a brief period before my departure to England.

I was a small child who was very quiet at school and being bright was considered to be the teacher's pet or teacher's favourite. These factors were viewed by some as a sign of weakness which meant being bullied at Denham Town All Age School. I recall once a girl fought and beat me up with my trousers falling to my ankles and that was humiliating. I can laugh about it now but it was not funny or a joke back then. However I cannot remember what caused this to happen in the first place. Norma Moncrieffe another student used to protect me from the relentless bullying. One of her friends Rudolph McBean was my classmate and being bigger in stature meant he shielded her and as a result I was secured protection as well. I hate bullying and I am sure that these events of suffering at the hands of bullies as a youngster helped to shape my life in championing the causes of injustice.

Despite the bullying I was viewed as a Casanova or Romeo which meant some of the girls were always attracted to me. This caused some jealousy and my form teacher Audrey Shepherd who I understand migrated to Canada took a liking to me and I to her.

Once in class she was describing something for the students and referred to the situation as 'like Maxie with handsome lips'. For me to still remember that all these years later shows how positive I viewed her teaching ability as well as her beauty and warmth. I was besotted by her intelligence and charm as she epitomized what a beautiful woman looks like and why I later in life fell in love and married my dear wife. The memory of that teacher singing to the class the song called *The Yellow Rose of Texas* of which the earliest known version is found in *Christy's Plantation Melodies. No. 2*, a songbook published under the authority of Edwin Pearce Christy in Philadelphia in 1853 still remains with me.

I used to love going to watch matinee films on Saturdays at Deluxe Cinema, Three Miles, Kingston. On other occasions to use a Jamaican phrase I 'skulled school' which is truanting along with some of my school friends. A group of us used to go to a beach called Hot and Cold in Foreshore Road, Kingston and close by were the Copra House and Brand Staff ice factory. At the Copra House we would get coconut that was baked ready to be processed for making coconut oil and other hair products. For those who have never had the experience of eating baked coconut, as we would say in Jamaica 'half of your life is gone' since it has such a wonderful taste and flavour.

With Jamaica being such a hot country, at the Brand Staff ice factory as the word implied a lot of ice was produced on a daily basis for consumption. However we were more intent on getting to the beach to frolic in the warm sea water. To this day I am unable to swim and regret not being able to do so.

On one of those trips I remember being knocked over by someone riding a bicycle and it really shook me up badly. My mother was contacted and I had to be taken home. Normally in those days one would get a beating for having left school to be gallivanting elsewhere as I was following others older than I. However my mother, bless her heart was so relieved that I had not suffered any injuries that I was spared any punishment. As a matter of fact the culture or tradition at that time in Jamaica was to beat children for even the most minor misdemeanours. Once my mother overheard a conversation when I was defending her against another child who said 'you mother'. It is a fact that in Jamaica no one gets away with cursing another person's mother and anyone who does that is asking for trouble. I remember swearing at the child because of her disrespect towards my mother who in turn proceeded to give me a beating for using profane language which was so ironic.

Marijuana or cannabis often referred to as ganja has in recent times been legalized as a drug in Jamaica for medicinal and personal use. I wonder how much the great late Jamaica reggae singer Peter Tosh in his rebellious song *Legalize it* which was also the title of his first solo album in 1975 after leaving the singing group Bob Marley and the Wailers had to do with influencing that outcome. I mention that because as a boy I had my first experience of smoking this illegal drug whilst a group of us visited a place called Back-A-Wall in Kingston and came across some Rastafarians in the late nineteen fifties relaxing and smoking from a Chillum Pipe. As impressionable youngsters we were curious on seeing what these adults were doing with lots of smoke emerging from the pipe. Each of us decided to participate with no coercion from the group of Rastafarians. I inhaled one puff or 'draw' from the Chillum pipe and that was enough to knock me out as it made me delirious. I remember this cannabis smoking incident as if it was yesterday.

School meals at Denham Town All Age School were not the best; we called it a nickname 'Bolus slush' which should give you an idea of how awful they were. Instead at lunchtime those of us who could afford it made the journey a short distance away to Tom's bakery to buy the freshly baked hot bread with butter. It was the most delicious bread one could ever imagine and my mouth is salivating just thinking about it.

Jamaican proverb: *'Duppy know who fi frighten'*.
Meaning: Bullies know exactly who they can abuse.

Chapter 2
My migration to England

'Do not be afraid or discouraged, for the Lord will personally go ahead of you. He will be with you; he will neither fail you nor abandon you.'
—Deuteronomy 31 verse 8.

At the age of 16 leaving the sunny island of Jamaica without my mother and sister and the impact of being in the so called 'Mother Country' was without the shadow of a doubt a major culture shock that I experienced. Bob Marley's song *By the Rivers of Babylon* where mention is made of being in a strange land springs to mind when I think back to leaving that abundance of sunshine in Jamaica in March of 1960 to reach England the motherland with the weather a stark contrast to what I was accustomed. It was far from being motherly as my mother who was left behind in my native country still resonated with me as the one and only earth mother that I had ever known and I missed her dearly. It took me ages to become acclimatised to the seasonal changes as on occasions it was not uncommon to experience spring, summer, autumn and winter conditions all in the space of a day. My father was now living in England with his wife and during the height of migration in the sixties it was customary for parents to send for their off spring and being the oldest son of my father's children it was decided that I should join him. Although I was first in the pecking order my mother apart from the emotional bond and attachment was happy for me to join my father and his wife in Birmingham. I can still vividly remember being on the deck of the *SS Begona* a Spanish passenger ship as it set sail for England. I saw The Blue Mountains, the longest mountain range in Jamaica with its highest peak of 7402 feet, gradually disappearing in the background whilst my mother and sister waved goodbye from the dock of No.1

pier. Because of my tender age being the youngest person on the ship I was chaperoned by Mr. Blissett for the three week journey as he was someone my mother knew and trusted. Just before I left Jamaica the music of the time which I remember to this day was Laurel Aitkin's *Boogie In My Bones* and Owen Gray's *Please let me go*.

I am not ashamed to admit that I cried buckets of tears for quite some time on the three week journey and those were not tears of joy but of sorrow as the thought of the bird having to eventually fly away from the nest at 16 is still a young age. To leave the creature comforts, love and support of my mother and my beloved country, sweet Jamaica to go to new and green pastures thousands of miles away was a daunting prospect filled with trepidation. In fact this was unknown territory that I was heading to and I was in for a rude awakening. I was immediately taken aback by the large number of white people that I saw in England as was not accustomed to that in Jamaica and no one really prepared me for this eye opening experience. Even my mother related her experience when she arrived in England later on of being shocked on seeing so many white people all around. Frantz Fanon, a Martinique born black psychiatrist and revolutionist who later adopted Algerian citizenship, in his book *Black Skin, White Masks* covers the issue of black consciousness thoroughly referring to negritude and the fact that most black people do not realise their skin colour until they are surrounded by white people hence this being all about their level of consciousness and awareness. I picked that up without any hesitation the moment I landed in this country coming from a predominantly black environment.

As the proverbial saying or idiom goes 'the grass is not always greener on the other side' because on arriving in Britain at Southampton docks I saw rows of houses with smoke billowing from the chimneys as fires burnt inside to keep the occupants warm. Such a sight made me assume that they were factories instead of people's homes. By now it was the month of April and I distinctly remember how bleak the weather was and a total contrast to the sunshine that I was so accustomed to in Jamaica.

From Southampton dock I travelled with the other passengers to Waterloo train station in London. Cold Harbour Lane in Brixton was where I first laid my head to sleep on British soil and the song by the British singer Paul Young, *Wherever I lay my hat that's my home* springs to mind. On reflection where I spent that first night in England is quite appropriate considering Brixton in South London has always been one of the hubs for migrants arriving from the West Indies and was always at the frontline of the struggles that black people faced over the years. Mr Blissett my chaperone on the journey from Jamaica was heading to Birmingham where my father also lived. However since the arrangement was for my father to meet me at my uncle's home in Brixton I was left in the custody of another passenger who already resided in that area and I stayed with his family overnight. My father missed the time of my arrival by a whole day. With hindsight that might be considered to be a good omen of what I did in later life as had he arrived on the correct day to meet me as planned I would possibly have made the trip to Birmingham then. The next morning I was given directions to get to my Uncle William which was not too far away.

Walking on foot I was amazed at the amount of traffic as I was not accustomed to seeing so many vehicles even in Kingston. Armed with my grip now better known as a suitcase, with all my personal belongings, I recall asking a black man on the street for help with the directions to my uncle's address. Because of my upbringing I referred to him as Mister to which his response was 'Listen son, in this country you do not refer to anybody as Mister'. Bearing in mind that I did not know his name I thought that would have been the polite way to address him out of respect. I was taken aback by this remonstration and that was yet another culture shock which has stuck in my memory all these years, as in Jamaica it was customary to address adults with titles such as Mister, 'Mass', Misses or Miss as a form of respect. He meant well and was very helpful in getting me to my uncle's home. Later that same day my father arrived from Birmingham to fetch me and we made the trip to his home at Cooks Road, Nechells, where my stepmother greeted me. As a married couple they lived in a one bedroom rented accommodation which formed part of a three bedroom property and I remained with them for a few weeks.

There is a saying that 'blood is thicker than water' as not being my stepmother's flesh and blood she in my view treated me less favourably than her own children. I remember visiting her in Old Road, Red Hills district near Spanish Town in order to see my father and my other siblings but as the saying goes, 'See me and come live with me' is a different ball game altogether. The treatment that I received at first hand whilst staying with her in Nechells, Birmingham as someone new to England missing my mother and wanting as much love, support and guidance in getting to understand the British way of life was not what I had expected and was far from ideal. She could in my view have treated me like her own son and be more hospitable as I was still only 16 and vulnerable. There was a lot of conflict and the relationship was fraught with difficulty and tension with my father caught in the midst. Ever since I can remember there was strong rivalry between my stepmother and my mother over many years. Unfortunately I had to bear the brunt of it which is a shame as I have feelings and should not have been used as a pawn in that saga.

My father had two children with my mother, two with another woman and a further three with his wife and all of his children were born in Jamaica. Given the circumstances he tried his best with all of us from a maintenance point of view and always acknowledged his responsibility to each of us. My stepmother had left her three children that she had with my father back in Jamaica and it became blatantly obvious that she was not happy with me being the first one to arrive on the scene. Eventually my father had to find alternative accommodation for me in Nechells in an adjacent property on Nechells Park Road. It was in an attic consisting of four beds and three other male adults were there taking it in turns to bring various women for sexual encounters. As an impressionable sixteen year old I would clearly hear but not see the sexual activity taking place during the night by pretending to be asleep. It was indeed a shock to the system and in this day and age such exposure would be classed as child abuse. I had to keep this to myself and share it with no one even though I found it to be rather uncomfortable.

During that time my father spoke to me about hygiene and cleanliness. He said 'You need to have a regular bath, you have to go to the Nechells Park Public bath, and you have to learn to look after yourself because no one else will'. Some people might wonder how on earth I can remember such words of advice to this day but it stood out at the time and it is something that I have never forgotten. My father was trying to show me the route to independence and survival and sadly overtime I have not followed through such poignant advice on the aspect of really looking after myself as some people have taken advantage of my kind heartedness and used it against me. I do have some regrets about not being more ruthless looking after myself as my father had implied, rather than constantly putting others before me.

Conscription into the British army was no longer a possibility as one of the ways forward for me to progress in terms of learning a trade as it had come to an end. Having left school in Jamaica without any formal qualifications my next move was to apply for a trade apprenticeship within the factories through the Labour Exchange now known as the Job Centre but was told that being aged 16 I was too old for such a position. Can anyone imagine hearing such rubbish? I deemed it as an excuse to prevent me as a young ambitious Jamaican youth from achieving one of my goals in life to learn a trade or skill and that it was tantamount to racism. To this day I regard that episode as my first encounter or taste of institutional racism with access being blocked on the grounds of my age and colour. My skin colour did not fit and one needs to bear in mind that the first Race Relations Act to give protection for black and minority ethnic people from the evil of racism was passed by the British Parliament in 1965, five years after my arrival in England. I was advised to become a labourer in a sheet metal factory which I gladly took on board hoping to learn the required skills of a sheet metal worker in due course. I was not familiar with British factory culture and resented having to make endless cups of tea for the other workers along with sweeping the factory floor. To use the cliché I was 'the only black person' working there and stuck it out for a few weeks before moving on to another labouring job.

Jobs back in the sixties were not hard to come by and on one occasion I was successful in obtaining three jobs in a day but all were labouring jobs as that was the main work offered to black people. It was a regular experience of mine to see other black people lined up outside factory entrances on any given day asking if there were any job vacancies. In many cases the answer was usually 'yes' but it was to sweep the factory floor as a labourer or be a machinist if one was lucky enough.

I recall what amounted to another clear example of blatant racism whilst working at a factory when one of my white colleagues wanted to know if I had a tail like a monkey. I was so shocked on hearing the question being asked as never before has that been raised as an issue. Due to being naïve at the time I just said 'no' but went and told Uncle Lenny, my childhood hero who was now living in Birmingham about the incident. His advice was to go and tell him to lift up his mother's skirt and look underneath it where he will see something like a monkey's tail. I did just that and was sacked instantly by the boss of that factory for using explicit language. Some might find that experience funny whilst some will question whether that white man and others with their ignorant and racist views would ever ask that of another black person again. On reflection I hope it has served as a lesson to him and others with such narrow minded racist opinions.

My wages amounted to the princely sum of three shillings and six pence a week and as a youngster it was considered sufficient for me to get by. Just one example of the cost of living in those days was the national dish of fish and chips being one shilling and six pence and I will always remember it was wrapped in newspaper which I found somewhat strange considering the ink is dirty and this is food I was meant to consume. Thank God the British fish and chips industry has moved on since then as it used to irk and annoy people from the Caribbean in particular about wrapping cooked food in newspaper which was deemed to be unclean. Another issue of cleanliness was seeing unwrapped bread left on the door steps of people's homes alongside bottles of milk and I struggled to get my head around such an awful concept viewing it as unhygienic. Caribbean people arrived in Britain from the end of the Second World War 1939–1945 in large numbers as migrants having been invited to help to rebuild the so called Mother Country and its economy. We have certainly since then taught the English the importance of cleanliness and hygiene as amongst our traditions, the idiom 'cleanliness is next to Godliness' is of paramount importance. I wholeheartedly subscribe to the notion of being clean is a sign of spiritual purity or goodness with the phrase first recorded in a sermon by John Wesley in 1778. However the idea is ancient and found in Babylonian and Hebrew religious tracts as well.

Although I have mentioned how easy it was to get a job in those days and one could leave a job today and by the next day find another, on occasions I was unemployed and turned to what was then known as the National Assistance Board for financial support. It is now called the Department of Social Security (DSS) and the financial benefit that one received was commonly referred to as the dole. I had an enormous sense of pride and dignity and whenever I became dependent on social security benefits redoubled my efforts to find gainful employment as surviving on pittance was not something that I relished.

I have always been a family oriented person and made sure to visit my dear Uncle Lenny his wife Aunt Iris and their only child, Peter in Saltley, Birmingham and used to enjoy their family hospitality. Because of the dynamics and unstable relationship caused by my stepmother sometimes supported by my father I also used to regularly visit extended family members in other parts of Birmingham such as Handsworth and Aston. I did a stint at the now defunct Wimpy Bar on New Street which was next door to the famous Odeon Cinema.

Bearing in mind that I arrived in Britain in 1960, just a year later in 1961 after my father had bought a family home in Hart Road, Erdington, his three children from the union along with his wife arrived from Jamaica that October to join him. I went to live with him, my stepmother and my other siblings. On one occasion at about aged 18 returning home later than expected from a party I was locked out. Despite my repeated requests to be let in, it fell on deaf ears but thankfully my brother Allan opened an upstairs back window which I had to climb through to gain access to my bedroom. This is part of my survival instinct and locking a young person out of their own home is cruel and no adult should ever contemplate doing that. That is the point when I had enough and made the decision to go to London where relatives treated me with more kindness and hospitality. Whilst there I lived with relatives in various locations including Battersea, Wandsworth, Clapham Common, Brixton and Stockwell and did not sit on my 'backside' doing nothing. Having always possessed a strong work ethic I found employment at Herbert Jenkins Book store in Piccadilly Circus as a stocker of the books and also as a sales assistant in the renowned J Lyons Cafeteria on Buckingham Palace Road, Victoria. I have always been one for hard work and grafting to make ends meet and can never be accused of being work shy.

Jamaican proverb: *'If yu mash ants yu fin im guts'*.
Meaning: People reveal their true colours when faced with pressure or hard times.

Chapter 3
Arrival of my mother to England

*'No, O people, the Lord has told you what is good, and this
is what he requires of you: to do what is right, to love mercy,
and to walk humbly with your God.'*
—Micah 6 verse 8.

I had always hoped and prayed that someday I would be reunited
with my dear mother who I adored. She arrived in England three
years after I had left her by the dock of No.1 pier in Kingston in
1960 and I was elated to see her. My sister was left in Jamaica and
joined us sometime later so the family was once again reunited.
What a difference this reunion was in comparison to our parting
company three years before, crying my heart out. If anything my
tears were now of joy at being able to hug and touch my mother
and hear her voice once more. I hardly wanted to let go of her and
also never wanted her to leave my sight. At the time I was living in
London and made the trip to Birmingham filled with excitement to
see her. I made frequent visits in between my work commitments
and work schedule at every given opportunity to see her and catch
up with the stories from our three years of separation as she had a
lot to tell me and vice versa.

My mother being new and a stranger to England was given a
helping hand by others in her quest to find employment soon after
her arrival. Factory work was easy to find and she too worked in
various factories for a number of years until her retirement. So in
essence she followed a similar path to me as a factory worker.

My mother stayed with Uncle Lenny and his family in Saltley
until she was able to branch out on her own. My parents remained
on good terms with each other over the years and that for me was a
blessing as they had the interest of my sister and I at heart. It was

during one of my visits to see my mother in Birmingham that for the first time I met the person who was later to become my dear wife. I had on that occasion brought one of my first cousins named Zenith age 7 to visit Birmingham. On visiting some friends in Handsworth at the house where two of my future wife's brothers lived, my eyes became transfixed on seeing the most attractive young woman sitting behind a Singer sewing machine using it with great dexterity. I discovered that her mother was a seamstress which nowadays is better known as a dressmaker. For me it was love at first sight as until then I had never seen such a beautiful person on the planet. She appeared to me somewhat shy and reserved and I too was known for being polite and quiet which some might find strange as far as the quietness quality is concerned. I went back to London with this young woman never being far from my thoughts. We exchanged details and stayed in contact. This meant that there were two strong reasons to visit Birmingham on a regular basis, the first being to see my dear mother and the second to see the beautiful young woman. Over a period of time our mutual friendship and admiration for each other blossomed in to love.

After a period of courtship I left my job in London and returned to reside in Birmingham so that I could be closer to the new love of my life. Eventually I proposed to her and to my great relief and delight she willing accepted the marriage proposal. We got married in Birmingham and apart from the wedding itself with my mother and father being present beaming with pride, I still have fond memories of the occasion. The wedding to my sweetheart also happened on the day of The Grand National, a National Hunt horse race held annually at Aintree Racecourse in Liverpool, England. First run in 1839, it is a handicap steeplechase over 4 miles 514 yards with horses jumping 30 fences over two laps and most people like to place a bet on it. I was no exception and had asked one of my brothers to place a bet for me on a horse called Red Rum which he duly did. Later he was able to signal to me at the wedding reception with an approving nod of his head on me enquiring if the horse had won the race. I discovered that it had done so at very good odds. Interestingly that horse has gone down in racing history in Britain having won this well known race on three occasions.

My mother never learnt to drive so my sister and I took it in turn to take her to church functions and other social events. As a devout

Christian she studied the Holy Bible at the Church of God of Prophecy where she worshipped and received a certificate in Bible Studies which she proudly displayed in her home. Even when drinking a glass of water or a cup of tea, my mother was known to always offer a prayer giving God thanks and praise and that I found truly remarkable.

The union produced two lovely children, our daughter and three years later our son and we are both proud of their accomplishments and achievements. My wife and I have been together ever since and she has given me support through whatever trials and tribulations that have come my way. I would change the popular saying 'Behind every successfully man there is a woman' to 'Beside every successful man there is a woman and vice versa' as in our situation it is a joint approach even if my wife tends to stay in the background and out of the limelight.

I had a good relationship from those early days with one of my wife's younger brothers who is now deceased. However the same cannot be said of one of the older brothers who for reasons unknown took a dislike to me as a person. He eventually left England, returned to Jamaica and became responsible for farming the family land.

Jamaican proverb: *'Humble calf suck di most milk'*.
Meaning: Humility is more rewarding than arrogance.

Chapter 4
Survival of the fittest

*'Don't be afraid, for I am with you. Don't be discouraged, for
I am your God. I will strengthen you and help you. I will hold
you up with my victorious right hand.'* Isaiah 41 verse 10.

'Survival of the fittest' is a phrase that originated from Darwinian
evolutionary theory as a way of describing the mechanism of natural
selection. Herbert Spencer first used the phrase after reading
Charles Darwin's *On the Origin of Species*, in his *Principles of
Biology* (1864). I agree wholeheartedly with Herbert Spencer's
stance that "This survival of the fittest, which I have here sought to
express in mechanical terms, is that which Mr. Darwin has called
'natural selection', or the preservation of favoured races in the
struggle for life."

Migration to Britain was highly encouraged after the 2nd World
War ended in 1945 with the British Government inviting its
Commonwealth citizens who were members of the British Empire
to come to the so called Motherland and rebuild the economy. That
is in essence the reason for the influx of Caribbean people who
made that journey as well as to improve their way of life.

I used to take any jobs that came my way in order to earn a living
such as labourer, factory worker, metal dye caster, welder etc as I
did not have a choice due to my lack of qualifications and also the
society in which we lived keeping black people at the bottom of the
pile or social ladder. Survival was the name of the game and I was
never one to sit idly by depending on state handouts which in those
days was a form of national assistance. Even with my humble
beginnings and background my mother had instilled in me a work
ethic so the idea of waiting on state benefits was never part of my
modus operandi. *Sitting on the dock of the Bay* the well known song

by the late singer Otis Redding was not part of my way of thinking. The lack of better job opportunities was in my view tantamount to racism and lack of equal opportunities in a white racist society as this was the period of the sixties, seventies and beyond. It begs the question why invite Commonwealth citizens to come and play their part and then treat them with such disrespect and contempt. Pope John Paul II got it spot on when he said 'A society will be judged on the basis of how it treats its weakest member'.

A council house is a form of public or social housing built by local municipalities in the United Kingdom and Ireland which came in to being from 1919 onwards after the end of the 1st World War. Even with the advent of council accommodation black people were at a major disadvantage in their efforts to secure suitable housing and often remained permanently at the bottom of the housing waiting list for those who managed to get on in the first place.

It defies all logic and beggars belief that a lot of black immigrants from the Commonwealth having been invited specifically to help in rebuilding Britain's flagging economy after the 2nd World War, now faced a major housing crisis as even private landlords placed signs in their windows stating, 'No Blacks, No Dogs, No Irish'. This was an affront to our dignity and self respect in making comparisons of black people with animals and refusing us accommodation based on our skin colour. This was blatant racism at its worst on open display. White supremacy has always viewed black people as sub-human for many years and this was being reinforced. Considering Britain's wealth was gained on the backs of the enslavement of black people from the African continent over the centuries, to now deny us the basic human right of a roof over our heads for shelter is unthinkable and reprehensible.

For awhile my fiancée and I lived in Worcester where our daughter was born as I was working in the factories in that city. Once there was a minor dispute with one of our private landlords who wanted us to vacate his property immediately which was quite a shock leaving us with no idea of how to find alternative accommodation. The landlord occupied a part of the house as the custom in those days was to rent individual rooms to different families. I explained to him that there were new laws in place by the Harold Wilson government as of that year 1964 to give protection to tenants from scrupulous landlords such as himself who was abusing the system of tenants' rights. Luckily I used to regularly pick up leaflets available at the Labour Exchange on a number of subject matters pertaining to citizens' rights which I read diligently and therefore knew that his actions were unlawful and illegal and told him so in no uncertain terms. He called the police to the property with the intention that they would support his stance of immediate eviction. A white male police officer arrived and heard both sides of the story. At first the police officer seemed to be taking sides with the landlord but on hearing my explanations in reference to the recent tenancy & housing rights, he took the landlord aside to explain that his actions of wanting to evict us would get him in to trouble as he would be breaking the law. So as a result he withdrew the immediate eviction notice thus allowing us more time to find somewhere else to live which we duly did.

There was little or no legal protection for tenants so exploitation was rife. Landlords were well aware of the plight facing people who had arrived from the Caribbean and elsewhere and who were desperately in need of suitable accommodation. 'Rachmanism' is a term coined and used to describe the actions of notorious landlords such as Peter Rachman who was based in Lambeth, South London and owned several properties. Sudden evictions without any notice were the order of the day and one had no recourse to seek justice or complain. It impacted mainly on migrants and as a result the Government of the day led by Prime Minister Harold Wilson felt it necessary to bring in legislation under the 1964 Housing Act to give protection to vulnerable tenants caught up in this dreadful exploitation by landlords some of whom felt they were untouchable.

The black community in Worcester heard through the grapevine what I had accomplished as a young man then aged 21 and others in similar situations came seeking advice from me. So technically speaking I was giving factual information on tenancy and housing issues from then. So it was not a surprise when later in life I championed the cause of homeless young people at a project in Birmingham where I worked as a Senior Project worker for 22 years prior to my retirement in 2008.

On moving back to Birmingham it was the usual merry-go-round of renting accommodation and the issues surrounding that. In those days it was different from now as most renting of rooms in private accommodation was done by word of mouth or through someone known to you.

During 1964 there was a general election held in Britain and the Conservative candidate for Smethwick which is now part of Sandwell allegedly coined the phrase, 'If you want a nigger for your neighbour vote Labour'. He defeated the Labour candidate Peter Griffiths in what was deemed at the time one of the most racist ever run election campaigns in Britain. It created a storm of protest at the level of blatant racism being displayed by the prospective MP who was supposed to represent all ethnic groups in the borough of Sandwell in the Houses of Parliament. This coincided with African-Caribbean and Asians living in the borough being denied access to public and social housing. This form of institutional racism and injustice prompted the Black American activist Malcolm X to visit Britain in 1965 and he came to Marshall Street, Smethwick to highlight the plight of what was happening in the borough and on that street. Malcolm X has been honoured with a blue plaque in Smethwick almost 50 years after he visited the West Midlands town during heightened racial tensions. The idea for the plaque was suggested by Nubian Jak Community Trust which organises Britain's only Black and Minority Ethnic national plaque scheme.

My mother was very proud when my sister had her daughter in August and our first born a daughter came in October the same year followed by our son three years later. She has always had a good relationship with all three of her grandchildren and that has followed through with her two great grand children. My mother's love for children has rubbed off on to me because for over fifteen years my wife and I have been approved foster carers for Birmingham Fostering and Adoption unit having done all the required training. We have fostered countless children on a short to long term basis and have thoroughly enjoyed welcoming various children of different ethnic backgrounds in to our family home despite obvious challenges that come with some teenagers. Some still keep in touch, regard us as their parents and it has been rewarding to see how children for whatever reasons deprived of love, care and attention, blossom in to well adjusted adults.

Whilst living in Worcester with my fiancée she travelled on a bus one day to meet me in the city centre. On the homeward bound journey I joined her on the same bus with the same conductress and driver. My fiancée paid her fare and found a seat. Shortly after I boarded the bus and also paid my single fare but the conductress refused to give me the correct change of one penny stating that the other black passenger who I was sitting beside had not paid the right fare on the earlier journey so she needed to recoup it from me without even ascertaining whether we were related or knew each other. She clearly took the view that since we were a young black couple sitting next to each other we were together. It was wrong of her to make such an assumption even though we were indeed a couple. However things got worse as she held on to my change and whatever had transpired earlier in terms of an underpayment of a bus fare had nothing to do with me. This developing situation was not about the penny change that I was rightly owed but the principle. I politely insisted that she hand over my change which she refused to do. She asked the driver to stop the bus and the police were summoned. The same white police officer who had previously come to assist the landlord at the property we were tenants in Worcester some weeks previously turned up and said 'Oh it's you again'. He asked me to come off the bus and I complied. He listened to my side of the story and also that of the conductress separately before ordering that she give me the change. He pointed out in a firm and clear voice when I embarked on the bus again, 'He knows his rights' which was a definite reference to both this and the previous housing rights' incident. I felt vindicated having stood my ground but was really annoyed that the bus was stopped and the police were called over such a trivial matter. So on receiving the change I threw it away in disgust as the entire situation had been blown out of all proportion leaving me feeling humiliated and belittled as a black man in full view of the other white passengers.

With the benefit of hindsight these two incidents involving the same white police officer on an eviction housing matter and the other on a bus in full view of the general public in Worcester in 1964 over fifty two years ago led me on a course of defending my rights and helping those who were less capable of defending themselves. Clearly that police officer admired and respected my stance and it must be acknowledged that unlike other major cities such as London, Birmingham, Liverpool and Manchester, Worcester is a rural town with fewer black people and this was more evident in the sixties.

This was definitely a sign of things to come as the following year whilst walking in the Worcester town centre a white police officer not in uniform approached me as well as another black man and requested that we both accompany him to the local police station because a crime had been reported. To this day I have no idea what was the alleged crime as he reiterated that we needed to be questioned. We both declined to go with the undercover police officer having done nothing wrong and it just reinforced from way back then how racial profiling and stereotyping of young black men going about their legitimate business were viewed with suspicion and targeted by the police simply based on skin colour. If we as two black men had complied most likely we would have been facing an identity parade for a crime that we did not commit and possibly ending up with 'trumped up charges' by a white police force that was clearly behaving in a racist way to decent law abiding black people.

On returning home to Birmingham, on occasions whilst heading home on foot from 'Blues Parties' in West Bromwich and Handsworth with my other friends in the early hours of the morning as we were not car drivers, the police frequently stopped and harassed us. They wanted us to prove our legitimacy under what, at the time, was the dreaded SUS law. In England and Wales the SUS law from 'suspected person' was the informal name for a stop and search law that permitted a police officer to stop, search and potentially arrest people on suspicion of them being in breach of section 4 of the Vagrancy Act (1824). However over a period of time it was disproportionately used in targeting members of the black community. The SUS law caused widespread public concern and major unrest and was abolished after the 1981 Brixton uprisings.

This idea of stopping and searching black people is not a new phenomenon as it has been happening from the sixties and beyond across Britain with that ethnic group from all the research data and empirical studies being disproportionately targeted in that regard. Having also often been the victim of racial discrimination at the hands of the police, it is a clear example of racial profiling based on skin colour. It was similar in a way to the South African apartheid of (1948 – 1994) a policy or system of segregation or discrimination on grounds of race. This finally led to Nelson Mandela's release from 27 years imprisonment on Robben Island in South Africa and him becoming that country's first black President. Apartheid was where black people had to prove who they were by always carrying repressive apartheid passbooks. Without the identity cards they were often arrested and imprisoned in a country where at that time over ninety percent of the population were black people. At one stage in Britain some politicians and others were clamouring for everyone to possess an identity card but that racist idea was finally abandoned in 2010 following a major outcry and vehement protests by civil liberty groups for all the obvious reasons.

From about age 21 I learnt to drive a car. However there were occasions when I drove without a driver's licence, without insurance, without road tax and a faulty hand brake which are all offences under the Driving License Act as governed by the Driving Vehicle Licensing Authority. Although I considered myself to be a competent driver at the time I had not as yet passed my driving test and my actions were unlawful and irresponsible.

After passing the driving test on my second attempt with the test costing only one pound then, I once was caught by the police driving under the influence of alcohol which is illegal in Britain if above 35 micrograms per 100 millilitres of breath. I was duly arrested and charged with a drink and drive offence. On reflection that was wrong of me to be breaking the law and I received a lengthy driving ban which proved inconvenient having become accustomed to driving almost everywhere. A hefty fine was also imposed by the court along with further penalty points on my driver's licence as my actions were indeed unacceptable. The exuberance of youth that I possessed, not thinking of the consequences of my actions but being of the view that I was invincible contributed to my anti-social behaviour. I strongly urge the youth of today not to follow this poor example of driving with excess alcohol as it is reckless and thoughtless and I certainly learnt my lesson the hard way from that foolhardy episode.

I recall prior to being banned for driving with excess alcohol on one of my 'nights out' playing games with the police as I spotted a patrol vehicle on my way home and knowing that I had drank too much alcohol whilst enjoying myself at a 'Blues party' ended up playing hide and seek with the cops. I do not know if they spotted my car but I managed to lose them, parked it and walked the rest of the distance. However the next day being a Sunday I had no recollection of where exactly I had left the car and spent all day until 4.00 p.m. trying to locate the vehicle only to discover it was close to my home.

On one occasion in my early thirties I went to a night club in Handsworth and after socializing for awhile met a couple who offered me a lift home to Yorkswood in Shard End for which I was grateful. The black male driver and his white female partner were in the front of the car whilst I was the only passenger in the back. It suddenly dawned on me even though I had drank some alcohol that he was not travelling in the right direction towards my destination and I became understandably somewhat agitated and concerned. I kept stating that he was not going the correct way so he became argumentative with his female companion who in turn started to argue with him. Eventually he stopped the car and I quickly jumped out as it was blatantly obvious that his intentions were far from honourable. I have never ran so fast in order to escape from the clutches of danger which had become apparent, and hiding out of view noticed that he kept circling to try and find me. I panicked and jumped over the nearest garden fence in order to avoid being caught and can only describe that man as a maniac. It was through the grace of God with His guardian angels offering protection that I was able to escape to tell the tale. It was truly a frightening experience which as a grown man I recall even now with a certain degree of trepidation. There is a clear message here about trusting strangers which needs to be taken on board and it is one that I would like to reinforce to all no matter how young or how old one might be as one must always be careful.

After several years of studying including at Bourneville College of Further Education (1979– 1982) I enrolled in 1983 as a full-time student on the Certificate Qualification in Social Work course (CQSW) at Birmingham Polytechnic now known as City of Birmingham University. However there was a build up to this eventually occurring.

Gordon Weaver who I have a lot of time and respect for along with his wife Biz developed the New Way access course for mature students. He was also a Birmingham University lecturer in Sociology and left an indelible mark on me as he stood for justice, equality and other social causes. He was passionate about these struggles and increased my desire and passion for fighting for racial equality and racial justice. During the daytime I was a labourer and store keeper at British Leyland the car manufacturer in Longbridge, Birmingham. However due to the high value of education instilled in me from an early age my thirst for knowledge led to the evening studies that I pursued.

Sometimes before night shifts I was able to find the time to attend the access course during the evenings twice a week and always attended despite the often abysmal British weather. I did additional studies alongside that access course and passed my GCE O/A level in History on World Powers in the 20th Century.

On completion of the New Way Access course in 1982 I obtained a certificate but was not accepted that year for the two year Certificate Qualification in Social Work (CQSW) course. So for a further year I completed the Community Certificate in Advice Work (CCAW) at Birmingham Polytechnic. Eventually after ten years I decided to take voluntary redundancy from British Leyland in 1983, a bold move at the time to finally start the CQSW course that academic year at Birmingham Polytechnic. Whilst studying full-time on a student grant I supplemented my income doing Youth and Community Work for Birmingham City Council at Small Heath Community and Shard End Youth Club.

The expectation whilst studying to become a social worker was that all students undertook three placements in different settings with the first and final ones being assessed. My first placement was at the Saltley office of the West Midlands Probation Service in Birmingham and that was successful. The second placement at a psychiatric hospital in Northfield focussing on mental health patients went smoothly. It has since been demolished and moved elsewhere. My final placement was at Area 5 Birmingham Social Services Department in the elderly team in Newtown. And so began my living nightmare. The white supervisor on this placement in conjunction with some of the white staff at Birmingham Polytechnic decided to fail me claiming that my work was not of the required standard. The process when one has failed a placement is a referral to the external examination board comprised of fourteen independent assessors. The final decision was that six voted for me to be awarded the certificate, five voted against and three abstained. Some of the panel members interviewed me briefly on the day of the hearing at Birmingham

Polytechnic and to my shock and surprise I was informed in writing at a later stage of the decision to fail me.

I had no option but to lodge an appeal against what I deemed a rather draconian and outrageous decision designed by a racist system to 'stitch up' me up and prevent me from practising my chosen profession. At this point I called upon Gordon Weaver my former Sociology lecturer from the Bourneville College New Way Access Course for his invaluable assistance. He was the only person in whom I had faith in his academic skills, ability and competence to challenge the institutional racism that I was being subjected to. He never let me down fighting tooth and nail for as long as he could but the entire system and odds were stacked against me. I felt as if I was being used as a guinea pig in a laboratory experiment.

Whilst the appeal was pending I was given the opportunity to do a fourth placement in Wolverhampton in a generic social services team for approximately four months travelling daily from Shard End in Birmingham to that location. I had three white female supervisors plus my white personal tutor which was overkill, over the top and unheard of. The message being conveyed was that it needed four white women to subdue my creativity and enthusiasm in order for me to conform to social work norms from a white perspective and in essence deny my existence, ethnicity and culture. All I ever wanted to do was stand up for the rights of others who did not have a voice and were being oppressed. I believe that their sole intention was to highlight the feminist agenda at the expense of being a black man and therefore they deemed me as sexist and needing to use their white power and control to mould me into their way of thinking. What they did not understand is that my God created me in His own image and that is indisputable and was never up for negotiation.

This was a recipe for disaster as there was no need for so many white people all female to become involved in my supervision. It was oppressive to say the least and in my view was their deliberate approach to silence me trying to succeed on my chosen career path as a social worker. They collectively stifled my creativity and not to my surprise ended up failing me for a second time. This all happened at a time when the white feminist agenda and movement in Britain were still quite popular and I felt the full force of that backlash. This brand of white feminism did not allow or cater for the empowerment and upliftment of black women in their struggles as white feminists would not equate any aspect of racism in their mode of thinking. My personal tutor was no exception as a white middle class woman who was known for her strong feminist beliefs. In some of our base group discussions which were only for students there was a lot of talk about women's liberation. The emphasis during my time at Birmingham Polytechnic was a perception of an institutionally racist establishment where women's rights and equality for women were of paramount importance with far less emphasis on racial injustice, racial discrimination and racial equality. These issues did not feature as often as it should and were not regarded as priorities even though black families in Britain were some of the most socially deprived, racially harassed, racially abused and racially victimised. What these white feminists failed to understand or grasp was the double disadvantage of racism and sexism that black women encountered due to their ethnic background and gender.

I was distraught and it had a devastating impact not only on me but also on my marriage as there understandably developed a strain in our relationship as a direct result of this so called 'failure'. After being 'failed' I was depressed as they had pulled the rug completely from under my feet and I had nowhere to turn to, with no job, no professional qualification and the student grant for mature students which I had survived on had now ended. Being a God fearing person from a traditional Christian background I often read some of the 150 Psalms of David which are ideal as a source of comfort, hope and relief during what were for me gloomy and lonely days.

One night I had a powerful dream seeing a Christ-like figure in the heavens looking down and giving me assurance that everything was going to be alright. I also dreamt of trying to escape from a terrible storm and whilst attempting to seek shelter ended up being locked out of a building. The imagery and symbolism of such a dream in 1986 some 30 years ago has stayed with me even to this day. It impacted on me to such an extent that I was embarrassed to come face to face with others who had studied with me over the years, using the defence mechanism and avoidance tactics of not engaging with them whenever I saw them in public.

To this day I will never forget the telephone call of support that I received on Christmas Day that year from Nancy Johnson a former

Probation Officer who later became a Senior Probation Officer and afterwards Head of Equality at the Women's Unit of Birmingham City Council. During that painful period for her to have taken time out to call me spoke volumes and showed the extent of her care and encouragement for which I remain truly thankful. Previously she had looked at all the relevant paperwork and course work regarding my so called 'failure' of the final placement and concluded that it was no worse than anyone else who had passed.

What helped me to recover from this awful and traumatic experience is the realization that perception is a two way process i.e. whether it is to do with an individual or an institution. It is my opinion that my colour, my approach, my frankness in addressing issues pertaining to racism and inequality which also reflected in my written assignments played a major role in their decision to fail me. If the truth be known I should be seen and not be heard or not rock the boat in order to get the qualification. In other words 'do not ruffle feathers'. My integrity, principles, values and traditions counted for nothing. My biological as well as my psychological self were being attacked by white lecturers who had the power to decide my future and livelihood.

A classical example of my written work was around the issue of trans-racial fostering and adoption which entails white middle class couples adopting or fostering black children mainly from the inner city. There is a plethora of research and empirical data which highlights the fact that however well meaning their intentions were the reality for these young black children being raised by white families especially in white suburbia was damaging as their culture, heritage and identity were lost and not properly focussed on. I was all in favour of same ethnic background placements and this did not strike a chord with the powers that be. A video produced at the time looking at the issue of black children in local authority care showed some of these youngsters being so ashamed of their skin colour that they tried in vain to scrub their black skin in order to become white. That is one of the most psychologically damaging things for a child of an impressionable age to have to deal with instead of being proud of their black skin. Racism is well and truly alive having distorted the thinking of these young black minds but it does not stop there as some black adults in some countries have developed the bad habit of bleaching their skin with dangerous chemicals in order to make their complexion fairer as a means they think of gaining acceptance in society. Their mentality in this regard truly beggars belief and shows a distinct lack of black consciousness and awareness and how they perceive themselves as black people.

In order to survive the blatant and subtle racism experienced on a daily basis in society I gained more strength, power and had a flame ignited in me to take this to another level. This constant adrenalin rush is similar to when someone faces danger and develops an unknown inner strength to see it through. Life for me has always been a case of fight or flight when appropriate and on most occasions I have chosen the former.

My wife was at the same tertiary institution doing the four year Sociology degree with a CQSW option which was different from the two year CQSW course I had embarked on. There was an overlap whilst we were both students there although we never attended the same lectures.

Out of every disappointment comes good or when one door closes another one opens so I took the knock on the chin like a prized fighter, got up, dusted myself off and changed direction. What happened was a blessing in disguise although I did not view it as such back then. I certainly would not have been able to be as effective as a human rights campaigner and activist whilst remaining within the constraints of a racist institution such as Social Services with all its flaws, lack of freedom, red tape, bureaucracy, power and control and no proper understanding of the impact of racism, oppression and keeping black people silent. Throughout my life I have never been one to suffer with the house slave mentality of being grateful and satisfied with the crumbs that fall from the master's table or being told how high to jump. In other words I am not one to be running at someone's beck and call just for the sake of doing so.

It took a great amount of time, energy and effort for me to get over the trauma and disappointment of not being able to practise as a social worker. Fully trained but being denied the certificate knocked my confidence but life had to continue. The thought of returning to the factory floor horrified me a great deal but I made a conscious decision not to do so considering my past experience and the conditions that black workers were being subjected to in such a hostile working environment. The subservience, menial mentality and treating black people as if we did not have any sense really angered me and I was not prepared to return under any circumstances. The main reason for trying to achieve the necessary academic qualifications was to escape those terrible conditions of the factory floor and show that as a black person I had drive, ambition and the capability of achieving so much more academically and other wise. My possible return to factory work affected me so much psychologically and was forever playing on my mind that on one occasion I even had a nightmare and woke up covered in sweat which in itself says a lot.

Jamaican proverb: *'Time longa dan rope.'*
Meaning: Time will right or avenge all wrongs.

Chapter 5
My work at a housing project in Birmingham

'In God I will praise his word, in God I will put my trust; I will not be afraid. What can flesh do unto me?'
—Psalm 56 verse 4

I began looking for gainful employment applying for various jobs in the care sector in Youth and Community Work which was one of my likings having that practical experience, studying and affinity with young people. I applied for jobs across the country, was shortlisted and attended many interviews. However I was not successful in obtaining any of those jobs until I got one in June 1986 as an advice and welfare project worker for homeless young people aged 16-25 in Birmingham City Centre. That project was the central referral point for the organization and it was a role that I embraced with enthusiasm due to wanting to help young people. It was a sense of relief now being able to earn a living wage to support my family.

The role enabled me to find accommodation for young people in the age group aforementioned who had become estranged from their families due to breakdowns in relationships. Referrals ranged from domestic violence, child abuse, incest, substance abuse such as alcohol, drugs, glue sniffing, male and female prostitution and mental health issues covering all ethnic backgrounds and social class. The support staff was like a walking encyclopaedia with a wide range of knowledge on social security benefits, welfare rights and housing issues along with providing counselling. Thus we were able to signpost homeless and vulnerable youngsters accordingly. The main source of referrals came from the Local Authority, Social Service, Youth Service, Probation Service, solicitors and the police as well as family, friends and the public at large. It was not uncommon for other voluntary community groups and individuals such as the local traffic warden to make referrals.

Alongside all of what I was doing to help young homeless people my wife and I were able to purchase our first mortgaged property six months after starting this new job. Having up to that juncture lived in privately rented accommodation followed by local authority council housing it was such a pleasure to be proud home owners for the first time. It was for me a great accomplishment as to be on the property ladder meant so much to us as a family. Here I was working with people who did not have a roof over their head and sometimes had to sleep rough on the streets or on a kind person's sofa for awhile, finally owning somewhere I could call my home. That shows how fortunate I have been and I give God thanks and praise for that achievement.

The casework was demanding, challenging but rewarding especially seeing some of the positive outcomes for these disaffected young people. I worked there for 22 years and retired on December 19th 2008 in the same position that I started on 9th June 1986. My job title on retirement was that of senior advice and welfare project worker which was in name only as despite all my Herculean efforts to be paid accordingly and given recognition for that role I never received any salary increases for all the additional responsibilities. Constantly deputising for the absent line manager, having completed level 4 National Vocational Qualification (NVQ) Housing Management and the approved Certificate in Housing Management at Birmingham University still did not bring about any further remuneration. During my twenty two years of employment at the homeless project it was not all smooth sailing as even though I was complimented and praised for all the work I did in helping young homeless people and increased the profile of the organisation I encountered difficulties as a black worker. I felt marginalised, victimised and deliberately passed over for promotion on numerous occasions even though I had the ability, knowledge and skills far beyond the job specification and as mentioned previously deputized for the manager on several occasions. I represented the organization externally and internally at meetings, seminars and conferences and defended its ethos in the public domain during times when it was subjected to a lot of adverse criticism especially within the black community. I held my ground and defended the senior management of that homeless project like a Praetorian Guard. However on applying for promotion to a senior managerial position I hit a stumbling block as despite being shortlisted I was not appointed.

They appointed another internal white candidate with less experience and less qualifications for a role that I was ideally qualified and suitable for. I actually taught that particular individual when he initially joined the organization in the same office how to do the job. He ended up being promoted, becoming my line manager simply because my immediate white line manager had a disliking for me and deliberately aligned himself with my competitor. He gave him all the support and mentoring so that he was successful in being appointed. That was such a kick in the teeth and also below the belt as it occurred at the same time I had lodged grievances against my line manager for failing to support me against racist clients who blatantly abused me over a period of time in his presence with racist names, such as 'coon', 'nigger' and 'black bastard'. On complaining his reply was 'What do you expect me to do about it?' Imagine hearing that response from your direct line manager who witnessed on more than one occasion the racist behaviour of some white clients towards me as a black employee. He never reprimanded or challenged us which would have been one of the most telling and powerful means of supporting me. By remaining silent his actions smacked of collusion and I was forced to take out a grievance dealt with by head office staff who just went through the motions and supported his racist stance.

What is rather disturbing is the fact that the organization had clear defined policies, practices guidelines and procedures on how to deal with racist behaviour from both clients and staff and my line manager adhered to none of those. He failed to have any regular staff meetings and supervision in order to address what I was experiencing as a black worker and regularly used the term 'throw it in the long grass' which meant forget about. He was actually empowering the racist perpetrators before my very eyes.

The homeless project that I worked for had the opportunity to second employees on full pay to study for the same two year CQSW course that I had apparently 'failed'. Being ambitious and knowing my capabilities I put in an application to be considered as one of those candidates with a view to doing the course again at another tertiary institution. Some might view that as me being a glutton for punishment but I saw it differently in that it was another opportunity to achieve my goal. I was not chosen so queried the selection process by asking a series of written questions about the composition of the panel, the criteria used for selection and the ethnicity of the applicants and the ones who were successful. I discovered that all of the seconded staff were white and that for me was a deliberate act of racial discrimination. I tried as is the custom to remedy this injustice by the internal grievance procedure and the Chief Executive Officer (CEO) did his utmost to prevent me from taking my grievance to the final internal stage. Even though an external independent panel comprised of a diverse ethnic group later found in my favour that the actions of my employers were racist and their equal opportunities policies were not adhered to, the CEO did not rectify the problem leaving me with no alternative but to lodge my first ever case at the Birmingham Employment Tribunal on the grounds of racial discrimination. I was supported by the trade union called the National Association of Local Government Officers (NALGO) now known as UNISON.

Prior to the actual Tribunal Hearing my trade union representative and I were able to negotiate an Out-Of-Court settlement. The anguish, pain and hurt this caused me cannot be quantified and is immeasurable.

After that Chief Executive Officer retired the new director said in one of our conversations that she had been told by her predecessor that I was like a 'dog with a bone' and would never let go of a situation. That amounted to blatant racial victimisation even though all I did was stand up for my rights, fair play and justice. This reinforced the struggles I had in seeking promotion internally in that organisation despite 22 years of dedicated, committed and faithful service as I was being labelled unjustly and unfairly because of the courage of my convictions. Life can be so cruel but it was during times like these that my trust in the Lord shone through.

Having received an accolade as the winner of the Prime Minister's Regional and National Active Community Award 2000 for building a fair and just community, the Chief Executive Officer who clearly took a dislike to me continued to show his malicious streak and intention by never acknowledging this achievement in the workplace. It was after complaining about his appalling behaviour and lack of judgement to his successor that she took the opportunity to write congratulating me on the accolade and also apologizing for not making this recognition known in the organization as a beacon of success.

Because of my high media profile within the community campaigning for social justice and equality and my role as a trouble shooter in the organisation sorting out clients and workers' problems, my belief is that the organization was reluctant to promote me even with the right skill set that I had clearly demonstrated. The continued racial victimisation that I was being subjected to, right until the point of my eventual retirement in 2008 meant promotion of any description no matter how well I performed in interviews was never going to take place. On occasions they made sure to include on interview panels other black senior managers who rubber stamped their racist behaviour. Do not be duped by the diverse representation seen on interview panels or jurors on jury service thinking they will ally themselves or empathise with your situation. The proverbial saying 'Not all that glitters is gold' springs to mind as some black people deliberately chosen to make panels diverse and ethnically mixed are lacking in an awareness of what the dynamics of racism is about and its' wider implications. Some black and minority ethnic people can be referred to as internalized racists who have taken on the values, principles and beliefs of a racist system without even questioning their role within it.

Having on a second occasion some years later exhausted the internal grievance process on another issue pertaining to racial discrimination and blatant lack of promotion I was left with no other choice than to lodge a second tribunal case against my employers due in principle to being constantly racially victimised. I had applied for the post of manager for the homeless project as my line manager who started in that position about a year after I commenced employment there in 1986 was about to relinquish his post due to retirement. It was the perfect opportunity for me to slot into this role permanently as I used to perform some of his duties and responsibilities whenever he was absent and was expected to do so because of my seniority. To have been overlooked after a competitive interview process and be deemed as second best against someone who I trained on the job some time before as a new recruit was an affront to my dignity.

I sought the help of my trade union UNISON that I have been a member for many years but was let down badly by them and their legal representatives who refused to give me full backing for the Employment Tribunal. On the first day of the scheduled hearing having chosen someone else to legally represent me it proved to be a mitigating disaster as the person failed to turn up claiming she attended a wedding the weekend prior to the Monday morning start of the tribunal. To make matter worse she claimed to have only received the paperwork that same weekend and did not have enough time to prepare for the case.

This was like a salmon swimming upstream against the tide and on being advised to withdraw my strong case had to do so reluctantly. I felt crushed and was very disappointed on so many fronts. Unfortunately it was only after my retirement a few years later that I discovered amongst papers in my possession that I had the relevant household contents insurance with legal protection cover that would have enabled me to employ a qualified legal team up to the value of £50,000 for representation at an employment tribunal hearing. It is very important for others who might find themselves in a similar situation to be mindful and aware of the policy of legal protection cover on their household contents insurance which is an optional extra as it proves that knowledge is power and was a bitter pill for me to swallow.

Jamaican proverb: *'Annu every kin teet a laugh'*.
Meaning: It is not everyone who smiles to your face necessarily means you well.

Chapter 6
My work at the
Birmingham Racial Attacks Monitoring Unit

*'But let justice roll down like water and righteousness like
an ever-flowing stream'.*
—Amos 5 verse 24.

During this period alongside the role aforementioned I realised that
there was a pressing and demanding need to enable, empower,
develop and support the black and minority ethnic community who
were under attack from racist elements within society. In a detailed
Home Office inter-departmental report produced in 1989 statutory
agencies such as the police, Social Service, Probation Service, the
local education authority and Youth Service were seen to be
insensitive and incapable of dealing with issues faced by the black
and minority ethnic community. The report was unequivocal in
stating that racial attacks and racial harassment were on the increase
and Birmingham was chosen because of the high percentage of
black and minority ethnic communities to be the location for the
Birmingham Racial Attacks Monitoring Unit (BRAMU) as an
independent organisation although funded by the Birmingham City
Council's Equality department.

The Scarman Report (1981) some eight years previously involved
a full scale inquiry in the uprisings of that period, which mainly
impacted on the lives, well being and struggles of black people also
concluded that racism was unintentional. In essence Lord Scarman
failed to acknowledge the wide spread racism that black and other
minority ethnic groups were experiencing on a daily basis. This
allowed some white people and some white led organisations to
continue their racist oppression of black people instead of
concluding in his findings in simple terms that white people were
racist due to their history and socialisation process and needed to

change their attitude, behaviour and negative way of thinking towards black people who they constantly stereotype. The racism black people are victims of is perpetrated by some white people.

As a result it was decided to set up an independent community based organization which would empathize and highlight the needs of the black and minority ethnic population and that led to the formation of the Birmingham Racial Attacks Monitoring Unit (BRAMU). I became heavily involved from its inception in 1989 and eventually was the Chairman for a number of years. However due to the rather short sighted, narrow minded and blinkered approach of the Birmingham local authority with the full support and backing of the Conservative government of the day without any thorough risk assessment a decision was made to permanently close a number of anti-racist organisations across the country in 2010 including BRAMU.

During BRAMU's 21 year existence over 5000 cases of various forms of racial attacks were dealt with. Referrals ranged from physical and verbal abuse, racial harassment, racial bullying, graffiti using racist language daubed on people's properties and excrement and racist literature posted through people's homes. As the Chairman of the organisation our offices in Birmingham as well as the Sandwell Racial Harassment unit in West Bromwich were not exempt from the vile actions of some of these narrow minded individuals.

Quite separately BRAMU over the years had a number of high profile cases that involved the police and prison officers. The unlawful killing of Alton Manning confirmed by a unanimous all white jury's verdict at Bromsgrove Coroner's court on 25th March 1998 whilst a remand prisoner at Blakenhurst privately run prison in Worcestershire on the 8th December 1995 was a major victory for the organisation. It came about as a result of a massive campaign and with several High Court hearings lasting three years before the unlawful killing verdict was reached. I was present throughout and saw tears in some of the jurors' eyes after the announcement was made. Although the prison officers, who according to the inquest verdict unlawfully killed Alton Manning, were identified they have never faced trial and may have questions to answer.

Clive Forbes a young black man on the 13th June in 1996 was pushed off a ledge near his home on the infamous Wryley Birch estate in Birmingham after suffering a lot of racial abuse from white racist perpetrators. That housing estate was regularly referred to BRAMU over a protracted period of time due to the high number of unprovoked racial attacks that black residents experienced at the hands of white perpetrators.

I visited Clive Forbes on behalf of BRAMU whilst he was a patient in Queen Elizabeth Hospital, Birmingham where he had a brain scan due to the extensive injuries he received from that racist attack. West Midlands Police force became heavily involved as that estate was notorious for their racial attacks on defenceless black residents and we had to give a lot of support to the victims. This victim wanted to move from the notorious area and be re-housed with his partner and that in itself was a major feat to accomplish. The policy of re-housing a council tenant by the local authority in 'like for like' accommodation was at times not adhered to so BRAMU as an organization had to fight the housing department in our efforts to get him suitable alternative accommodation elsewhere. When someone has been racially attacked and racially abused it is the norm and policy of the local authority's housing department in Birmingham to give support to the victims if they are council tenants and go as far as evicting the racist perpetrators from their council accommodation. It has been known to work to great effect and one must not lose sight of those practice guidelines and procedures pertaining to a tenant's eviction for racist behaviour towards other residents who are often black or from another minority ethnic group.

Although BRAMU was a Birmingham based organization referrals came from other areas of the country where no such facilities existed for people on the receiving end of racial violence, racial harassment and racially aggravated offending. Deaths in custody, wrongful arrests, stop and search were also areas of major concern that impacted on black and other minority ethnic groups warranting our support and intervention which were duly taken on board.

There were racist death threats against victims and also against me as the Chairman of BRAMU. These had to be reported to the West Midlands Police for investigation and the white racist culprits were identified and dealt with. Even at the point of closure in 2010 BRAMU had 120 cases and to this day it still hurts having to tell those victims that we could no longer help them. It needs to be made abundantly clear that the service BRAMU provided over the years reflected our diverse board of directors, its work force and the clientele group in that it represented all ethnic groups including white people. It was truly cosmopolitan, ethnically diverse and kaleidoscopic along with being very effective in its approach.

The major role of BRAMU was to monitor the trends of racial harassment which involved providing accurate data and factual reports for the local authority and the government in order to help stem the tide. Also of paramount importance was to casework the victims by offering them practical support such as accompanying them to Courts, hospitals, clinics, neighbourhood offices, schools, police and solicitor interviews and wherever else deemed appropriate. The significance of all this important and detailed work is sadly no longer available so black and minority ethnic groups in effect have nowhere to turn for advice and support.

Rebecca Wood's review of April 2nd 2009 in the Institute of Race Relations (IRR) report, 'Can Community Campaigns against racism survive the new funding regime' was explicit about the impact the closure of BRAMU would have on race relations and the clientele group. Some august bodies such as the 1990 Trust, The Runnymeade Trust, Liberty, Operation Black Vote, the London based Newham Monitoring Project along with BRAMU highlighted the fundamentally flawed concept embossed in the 2010 Single Equality Act bringing all the strands of race, sexuality, disability, age, gender, religion/belief together. They remained adamant that race needed to stand on its own given that most research pointed to racism being the major contributing factor for attacks but that has been ignored to the detriment of all victims of racism.

There was a resurgence of far right racist groups such as the British National Party (BNP) and the National Front (NF) along with infiltration by the American Ku Klux Klan (KKK) in 1989 after the uprisings in several inner cities such as London, Bristol, Birmingham, Liverpool and Manchester concerning social conditions as well as police brutality and police harassment of black youths. As a result anti-racist organizations aforementioned along with Marc Wandsworth's Anti-Racist Alliance and the black sections in the Labour Party had to counterbalance that threat and become more proactive in dealing with it.

The lives of thirteen young black people were prematurely ended by a fire which occurred at a house party in Deptford, London in

1981 triggering one of the biggest marches seen in Britain organized by the black community. To this day no one has ever been charged or brought to justice for what have been deemed as racist murders. "13 dead, nothing said" still remains the campaign slogan after all these years.

The tragic death of Cherry Groce on the 28th September 1985 by officers from the Metropolitan Police Force using their guns to shoot her in her Lambeth home in South London whilst they were searching for her 21 year old son in relation to a suspected firearms offence triggered the Brixton uprisings which spread to other inner cities across the country. In March 2014 some 29 years later the police eventually apologized for the wrongful shooting of Cherry Groce and in July of the same year an inquest jury concluded that eight separate police failures had contributed to her tragic and untimely death with the Commissioner of the Metropolitan Police Force, Sir Bernard Hogan-Howe apologizing unreservedly for its failings to the family.

Joy Gardner was a 40-year-old Jamaican mature student living as an undocumented migrant in London who died following an attempt by police officers to detain her for deportation. During a police raid on her home in Crouch End, London she was restrained with handcuffs, leather straps and gagged with a 13-foot length of adhesive 'Elastoplast' tape wrapped around her head. Unable to breathe she collapsed and suffered brain damage due to asphyxia. She was placed on a life support machine but died following a cardiac arrest four days late on 1st August 1993. In 1995 three of the police officers involved stood trial for Joy Gardner's manslaughter but were acquitted.

I have chosen specifically to highlight the fact in the aforementioned paragraphs that the racism of the far right seemed to sit comfortably alongside police brutality being ever present in British society for the longest while with the problem being ignored as the system is designed to maintain the status quo.

Following the Sir William McPherson inquiry into the racist murder of 18 year old Stephen Lawrence by a group of white racist thugs whilst he was waiting with his black friend Duwayne Brooks at a bus stop in Eltham, South East London on 22nd April 1993 the conclusion reached was that the police force in Britain is institutionally racist. I steadfastly maintain that remains the case even to this day. However due to the changes in British legislation double jeopardy has been permitted in England and Wales in certain (exceptional) circumstances since the Criminal Justice Act 2003. Double jeopardy means one can be charged and face trial a second time for the same offence. This meant that two of the five alleged perpetrators who were initially charged with murder but had the charges dropped, finally faced justice. With so many twists and turns over the ensuing years too numerous to document here two of the white perpetrators have subsequently been found guilty of the racist murder and are now serving life sentences imposed in 2012 some 19 years since the heinous crime. It makes me think of the famous quote by Thomas Jefferson who wrote the American Constitution, later used in his memoirs which said 'I tremble for my country when I reflect that God is just and His justice will not sleep forever.'

Deaths in custody in the United Kingdom in an ironic way is close to my heart as for many years I have developed a keen interest and a passion for supporting bereaved families and friends of people who have been unlawfully killed in police and prison custody. As a leading activist and campaigner over the years I have been instrumental in mobilizing public support, organizing marches, rallies, vigils, peaceful demonstrations and protests, representing distraught families as well as signing petitions highlighting social inequality and injustice on several fronts in relation to these tragic deaths.

Prisons, police stations, Crown Prosecution Service (CPS), Courts, Independent Police Complaints Commission (IPCC), Home Office, Government Ministers, MPs, local councillors, the media, the legal profession, community groups, human rights groups and the now disbanded Commission For Racial Equality (CRE) have either been lobbied or made aware of the need for justice to be seen to be done on this vexed issue of deaths in custody.

The heavy handed approach and use of unlawful force when dealing with black men in particular and the unauthorised restraint methods remain serious cause for concern. I have attended several inquests in Coroner's Courts throughout Britain and am always left shocked when the circumstances including horrific medical and pathological evidence of most of these unnecessary deaths are revealed in the presence of the Coroner, witnesses, the jury, bereaved family and friends.

I find it absolutely amazing that after all these years of so many deaths in custody it becomes like a stuck record where the powers that be say sorry, which is not in my view really meant and claim to have learnt from the errors of their ways. Some make reference to having undertaken further training on restraint methods but still continue to behave towards black men in particular as if they are not human beings with feelings and emotions deserving of dignity. Often black people are viewed by the powers that be as collateral damage but there comes a point when 'enough is enough'.

Some of this work has been achieved under the banner and umbrella of two national organisations in Britain, namely INQUEST and United Family and Friends Campaign (UFFC) alongside the work done by BRAMU and Sandwell Racial Harassment Unit. INQUEST is a small charitable organisation founded in 1981 whilst the United Family and Friends Campaign (UFFC) is an organisation which devotes a lot of time and energy to the families and victims of all ethnic people who have tragically lost their lives while in police and prison custody.

I have chosen to mention four young black men who all lost their lives under tragic circumstances whilst being restrained either by the police, prison officers or security guards in England:

1. *Alton Manning* aged 33 died in HMP Blakenhurst 8th December 1995. Unlawful killing verdict. The inquest into the death concluded on 25th March 1998 at Worcester and Dudley Coroner's Court (sitting at Kidderminster Town Hall) and the jury reached a unanimous verdict of unlawful killing. I was the Chairman of this campaign.

2. *Mikey Powell* aged 38 died in police custody in Birmingham 7th September 2003. Actively supported this campaign.

3. *Julian Webster* aged 24 died April 2009 outside a Manchester night club. In this case it was the security guards often referred to as bouncers who used their power and control far more than they should have done. Following the damning narrative inquest verdict of 25th May 2012 at Manchester Crown Court the campaign team is still waiting the Crown Prosecution Service (CPS) response to a judicial review granted by a High Court

judge, May 2014 in Birmingham. Current Chairman of this campaign.

4. *Kingsley Burrell* aged 29 died in police custody in Birmingham 31st March 2011. Past Chairman of this campaign and a judicial review is still pending.

These tragic and avoidable deaths and the Stephen Lawrence campaign where the ultimate has also been loss of life are moments that cause me immense pain, grief and anger. If only one could turn back the clock and erase all of these deaths from the annals of history so that they did not feature in my memoirs I would certainly do that in an instance as dignity and respect for all human life should be of paramount importance.

Martin Luther King Jnr once said 'An injustice anywhere is a threat to justice everywhere' and that makes it even more important for police officers, prison officers and security guards to be held accountable for their actions as no one is above the laws of the land.

The entire process of getting to the truth regarding these deaths in custody is long drawn out and frustrating when dealing with the British legal system and I make it a duty of mine to always explain to the parties concerned that it is not a sprint race but a marathon in order to prepare them for the long haul for justice. I have witnessed on many occasions at the end of that period that there is no guarantee justice will prevail even though the British legal system is reputed to be the best in the world. Surely someone needs to be held accountable and responsible for their actions. 'Justice delayed is justice denied' is a legal maxim meaning if legal redress is available for a party that has suffered some injury but is not forthcoming in a timely fashion it is effectively the same as having no redress at all and that is so apparent in some of the deaths in custody cases previously referred to. The time span of over twenty-seven years in the recently announced unlawful killing verdict of 97 Liverpool football supporters in Hillsborough Stadium from 1999 which highlighted the police corruption and cover-up is another case in point.

Attending several inquests at Coroners' Courts throughout the country over the years and appeals at the High Court along with the delay tactics, the gamesmanship of some involved in the Criminal Justice System with their failure to prosecute especially concerning black deaths in custody, has left me feeling at times demoralized and disillusioned. Witnessing firsthand the pain and suffering of the victims' families and friends adds to my sense of grief and despair but I will state unequivocally that I have no intentions of giving up this ongoing struggle for justice and equality.

I am consciously aware of the new initiative called #Black Lives Matter which has been making global headlines in the United States of America since the summer of 2013 after George Zimmerman's acquittal for the shooting death of 17 year old Trayvon Martin. Black Lives Matter (BLM) is an activist movement, originating in the African-American community that campaigns against violence toward black people. BLM regularly organizes protests around the deaths of black people in killings by law enforcement officers, issues of racial profiling, police brutality and racial inequality in the United States Criminal Justice System. The movement began with the hash tag #BlackLivesMatter and was co-founded by three black community organizers one of whom Patrisse Cullors, I had the pleasure of welcoming to Birmingham in 2015 when she visited England for a number of speaking engagements. She did a presentation at The Drum, an arts centre in Birmingham where I was one of the guest speakers on the panel for the Ferguson to Birmingham Campaign. We also hosted a reception for her at my local place of worship, Cannon Street Memorial Baptist Church in Handsworth.

With due respect a lot of my work and focus over the years in the struggle for justice and equality is similar to the #Black Lives Matter agenda and although I appreciate and do like the coined phrase as it does focus the mind, it is not a new phenomenon. However what I object to most strongly on my Facebook page is seeing comments denouncing the slogan and claiming that it should be #All Lives Matter which is stating the obvious. Of course in the grand scheme of things all lives do matter but considering the ones on the receiving end of police brutality, unlawful killings, oppression, wrongful arrest and incarceration often for the slightest misdemeanour or going about their business in all innocence are mainly black people, then the slogan is quite appropriate. It should resonate with conscious and forward thinking people from all ethnic backgrounds.

It is insensitive and offensive when leading politicians and other government officials across the globe such as the ex Mayor of New

York, Rudy Giuliani claim that #BlackLivesMatter is 'inherently racist' adding that black people need to teach their children to respect the police. So in essence he is blaming the black victims for their plight and affirming that the police are not at fault for shooting them. What about the police being less trigger happy in shooting and killing innocent and unarmed black people as if they are less than human? It is almost tantamount to a shoot to kill policy. At this juncture I need to make it crystal clear that I do not condone the killing of any innocent people as a means of retaliation.

One could easily argue that the enslavement of a large number of my African ancestors along with the notorious slave trade route from Africa to the West Indies and the Americas still reverberates on the #Black Lives Matter movement for reparation. The legacy and pain that is still endured from that era remains raw even now with the passing of time. The former Prime Minister of Britain David Cameron visited the land of my birth, Jamaica in 2015 and had the audacity to say the country should forget about the atrocities of the slave trade and the enslavement of my African ancestors and in essence move on. He also remained opposed to any meaningful reparation. Does Britain ever forget about commemorating the number of fallen soldiers in both World Wars? How would he like being told that Britain should forget about its war dead?

Jamaican proverb: *'Evryday buckit a guh a well, one day di battam mus drop out'*.
Meaning: If you repeatedly take the same risk, eventually it will end up in disaster.

Chapter 7
My work and involvement in Sandwell

*'Any Kingdom at war with itself is doomed. A city or house
divided against itself is doomed.'*
—Matthew 12 verse 25.

Alongside my work at the project for the homeless young people
in Birmingham I worked in a voluntary capacity in the borough of
Sandwell over a lengthy period of time. Voluntary organizations
that I helped to either form or had involvement with are as follows:

• Sandwell Ethnic Minority Umbrella Forum, SEMUF
  —Deputy Chairman.
• Sandwell African Caribbean Consultative body, SACCB
  —Chairman.
• Sandwell African Caribbean Forum Housing Project, SACF
  —Founder Chairman.
• Sandwell Racial Harassment Unit, SRHU
  —Chairman.

My reason for becoming so heavily involved was that the Sandwell
Metropolitan Borough Council did not have a single person of
African-Caribbean descent in local authority political representation
even at the start of the Millennium. That was alarming and disturbing
considering Sandwell which borders Birmingham, the second city,
at that time had a population of approximately 300,000 of which
10,000 were African-Caribbean.

Three of the aforementioned groups SEMUF, SRHU and SACF
were funded by Sandwell Metropolitan Council to aid and enable the
development of black and minority ethnic communities in the
borough. The other was of a voluntary nature.

Being rather frustrated at the lack of black political representation in the borough and as the only black person attending my ward meetings I wrote to Diane Abbott, Britain's first black female Labour MP of Jamaican heritage, representing Hackney, London. I explained to her the struggles and issues of one black voice with very little support crying out in the wilderness. She responded in a positive light which was encouraging as I was so disillusioned by the lack of participation, apathy and inertia of Sandwell's African-Caribbean residents.

A classic example of their reluctance to engage in the political process was demonstrated clearly when the late Bernie Grant as the then Labour MP for Tottenham, London was invited to be the main speaker at West Bromwich Town Hall in Sandwell. His topic was 'Black Political Representation and Engagement in the Borough.' Sandwell African-Caribbean Forum Housing Project made concerted efforts to mobilise our community to attend and having produced 5000 leaflets circulated them widely at betting shops/bookmakers, pubs, restaurants, barber shops, hairdressers, community centres, as well as publicising the event frequently on the local radio station. In a packed West Bromwich Town Hall I could count on both hands the number of African-Caribbean people who attended. This apathy and inertia can wear one down and make you question why bother. Later the excuse I heard from some African-Caribbean people was that they did not know about the event. At no stage despite all these setbacks did I ever contemplate giving up the struggle.

It followed that the ward in which I lived nominated me at the branch level as the prospective Labour councillor to go forward for selection. For the first time I tasted a whim of being in a political arena as a politician. However that did not materialize as unsurprisingly the members of the ward of whom the vast majority were white chose to select one of the white candidates. One of the active members who eventually became a councillor along with her husband later mentioned that to nominate me as a black person would have been a risk because previously an Asian person was selected for the ward and lost to another political opponent at the polls. This chain of events happened soon after the shock defeat of a black barrister John Taylor standing for the Conservative party in the 1992 General election in a safe seat with a 10,000 majority in Cheltenham a predominantly white area. It was because of racism and his skin colour that diehard Conservative voters chose not to vote for him and it was pathetic to hear him conclude that his heavy defeat had nothing to do with either. Black Britain was shocked and dismayed by John Taylor's denial. As an Operation Black Vote (OBV) website article of 26th January 2011 concluded, 'Racism in Britain during the 90's was ever present but it was always denied by the Establishment. This was the black community's moment to remind the nation of what black groups had been suffering on a daily basis. Taylor denied himself and his community of that moment.'

The journey in establishing and being involved with my hands-on approach in these aforementioned groups was one of the most challenging, difficult and frustrating experiences of my life. How I managed to keep my sanity God only knows. The idea of dealing with so many different cultures and all that entails along with the politics of the various groups and individuals were at times a recipe for disaster. Discussions in some of the forums were sometimes hijacked by others with different and personal agendas and cultural norms including the exclusion of women from participating in the democratic process. I had major problems with this as it went against the entire grain and ethos of what equal opportunity policies mean and represent. To deny women their fundamental rights bearing in mind everything that I stand for left me feeling rather uncomfortable as I constantly fight their corner to enable better representation.

During that period I wrote a letter to the secretary of the Sandwell Labour Party group highlighting the under representation of African-Caribbean people on the Sandwell Metropolitan Borough Council. His response was weak and not worth the paper that it was written on as he seemed rather dismissive of black people's struggles. On another occasion I wrote to the same secretary of the Sandwell Labour Party group having been a member for many years reiterating the same issue pertaining to the need for African-Caribbean representation. Yet again and unsurprisingly his response was dire, abysmal and unhelpful as to the way forward.

My memory of attending ward meetings was of being isolated, feeling as if I did not belong, coupled with a lack of genuine warmth. The well known Jamaican saying 'who feels it knows it' aptly describes my sense of exclusion instead of inclusion and not valuing my input. My local ward branch of the Labour Party was clearly not immune to racism which I experienced in a subtle way as described above because whenever I raised any issues pertaining to it they were just brushed under the carpet or thrown in the long grass. At one stage I wrote to my local branch ward secretary, via recorded delivery, requesting the opportunity to shadow him in his role but never got a response. After making enquiries with the administration staff I was informed that because I had sent a formal letter to him which was therefore on record he chose to ignore it. According to the member of staff he felt challenged or intimidated by anything in writing. I was not really accepted in the ward and felt that my presence was tolerated rather than being valued and embraced. On two separate occasions I had no alternative but to withdraw my membership from the Labour Party and only recently rejoined in 2016. John Spellar the current Labour MP for Sandwell has been representing that constituency for a number of years and once mentioned remembering my name because he always checked the list of people who left the Labour party and rejoined. Every Christmas without fail I received a card from him which stopped after my membership ceased.

It is of paramount importance that I explain the difference between each of the four aforementioned forums. SEMUF was the first of the four to be established as an umbrella forum in 1998 with it being the overarching body for all the black and minority ethnic projects. The others fed in to its remit and had representatives from other black and minority ethnic groups.

All the black and minority ethnic (BAME) groups had their individual forums hence the Sandwell African Caribbean Consultative body (SAACB) was developed to serve that community and I was selected to be its Chairman. This was the second of the four forums and meant that the other African- Caribbean projects were expected to feed their issues, aspirations and concerns into this body. The groups included were Sandwell and District West Indian Community Association (SADWICA) Community Action Project (CAP) The Tipton African Caribbean Forum, Organisation for Sickle Cell Anaemia Research and Thalassemia Support (OSCAR) and The African Caribbean Resource Centre. As the Chairman of the Sandwell African Consultative body (SACCB) I encountered some problems due to a clear lack of unity and cooperation amongst some of the groups who were all funded and financially supported by the

Sandwell Local Authority. However this consultative body was like a figure head with no power or financial backing. There was a split in terms of how some of the groups envisaged the direction and development that SACCB should take. At one point some members attempted to remove me as the Chairman but four other members and in particular Bob Cohen remained loyal. The renegade group tried their very best to get rid of me and eventually having fought like a trooper we reached a compromise with me stepping down. One of the main reasons for resisting their approach of wanting me to relinquish the role as Chairman was the undemocratic way in which they imposed their demands on me. I refused to give in to what amounted to a form of dictatorship almost like a coup d'état.

The third group, Sandwell African Caribbean Forum Housing Project (SACF) came about as a result of the dire need evidenced by research findings for a housing project to aid the African-Caribbean young people in the borough. So SACF in conjunction with Focus Housing Association, now called Midland Heart supported by Sandwell Council developed the Rolfe House Project, Rolfe Street, Smethwick with suitable accommodation for them. This project was officially opened by John Spellar, MP on 1st March 2002.

During this period there was a major rise of racial attacks throughout Britain, and Sandwell with its very diverse ethnic community was no exception as communities were suffering the brunt of this vicious assault of racism, by ultra-right nationalist groups who always seek to alienate black and minority ethnic groups. Tipton was one of the major trouble spots. Because of my experience and existing role at the time in the Birmingham Racial Attacks Monitoring Unit (BRAMU) I was asked to become the voluntary Chairman of a newly formed group known as the Sandwell Racial Harassment Unit (SRHU) set up by Sandwell Council: the fourth group to emerge. The unit had three full-time workers i.e. a co-ordinator, a caseworker and an administrative worker along with several volunteers. The casework was wide and varied with referrals from the Housing Department, Citizens Advice Bureau, Neighbourhood Offices, schools, Social Services, West Midlands Probation Service, the police and others too numerous to mention. The referrals were in essence similar to those I was accustomed to dealing with at BRAMU and none of the issues came as a surprise to me.

I recall as Chairman of Sandwell Racial Harassment unit receiving several death threats from right-wing fanatics who were trying to silence us as an organization and me as an individual from speaking out. This seemed to be a case of déjà vu as I had similar experiences of racist death threats as mentioned earlier at BRAMU. The unit's motto to all the clients who sought our help, advice and support was 'never suffer in silence' so the death threats aimed at keeping me quiet were a contradiction in terms of what the unit stood for. I remained undaunted and continued the task of helping the victims of racial harassment. My support throughout all of these trials and tribulations was from my family and others who stood for equal rights and justice and ultimately my Christian faith in my Lord and Saviour, Jesus Christ.

It was during this time, September 2000 that I was faced with an Employment Tribunal brought by two black women employed by the Sandwell Racial Harassment Unit who accused me along with the co-ordinator and the other board members of racial discrimination and sex discrimination. I have never been so appalled facing such allegations having always considered myself to be at the forefront of defending and standing up for people's rights and justice from a racial dimension and a gender perspective. I am a great believer in gender equality so to be faced with answering these charges at a tribunal left a bitter taste in my mouth.

Sandwell Council funded the defence cost of the Tribunal Hearing to the princely sum of £20,000 and we were represented by the well known black barrister Peter Hebert who is the current Chairman of the Society of Black Lawyers. The fact that unknown to these two women I championed their corner to be appointed in the first place based on their interviews makes it so ironic about what they did several months after their appointments. I was on the interview panel along with two other board members who were not of African-Caribbean descent. I clearly saw the potential these two women brought to the table and fought tooth and nail with the two panellists for them to accept that they were the best candidates for the two jobs on offer at the time. To this day they were never made aware of this and that hurts even more when the result of the contested hearing by an all white panel found us guilty of sexism but not guilty of racism.

From all of the anti-racism training I have been part of over the years, the starting point for me is that all white people are racists. It is with that in mind one of the black women who was married to a white man viewed the comment as offensive even though it was misconstrued and taken out of context. The comment was dealing specifically with casework and how it related to racism and police brutality, so for someone to have given evidence using that blanket statement was hitting well below the belt and unjustified.

To stand in a Tribunal Hearing being accused as a black man of being racist by two black women was incredible. My understanding is that we all have varying degrees of prejudices as a result of the socialization process, i.e. learned behaviour. However for a black person to accuse another black person of racism is illogical and not possible in my opinion. In its simplest form a definition of racism is prejudice + power + colour = racism and black people are not in positions of power.

I am not ashamed to state that during this traumatic Tribunal Hearing I broke down on the stand and wept uncontrollably because of what I was being accused of which is so far removed from the way I operate and my entire Christian principles, values and belief system. I will always remember seeing the hurt and pain etched on my mother's face as she watched and listened in that court room offering me her support whilst clutching her walking stick that she used to aid her movement. During one of the breaks I was still upset in the corridor and she raised her walking stick in a non threatening way and said as a form of motivation to me 'My son does not cry, my son does not cry'. I interpreted that to mean I am to wipe away my tears and fight like a man. When I reflect on this incident it makes her missing presence in my life so much harder to bear.

There was a sense of treachery of an ex-board member from a different ethnic background. He had taken a dislike to me simply because I had a justified cause to rebuke him regarding taking sides with employees without knowing the facts. It culminated in him now having the perfect opportunity at the tribunal to level the score so to speak as he gave evidence against me. In a biblical sense the actions of Judas Iscariot who betrayed Jesus Christ for 30 pieces of silver springs to mind, even though I dare not compare myself with my Lord and Saviour, Jesus Christ.

We were not found guilty on any aspect of racism and for that at least I am more than relieved as without a doubt that was the right decision. However the panel found us all guilty of sexual discrimination which meant myself, the co-ordinator and six board members were required to pay compensation to both women. At no stage did I ever intentionally discriminate against anyone or collude with any such behaviour with regard to sexism or sexual discrimination.

For the two black women workers this unfortunate episode which impacted on their lives is regrettable although it was not of my making. The day to today running of the Sandwell Racial Harassment Unit with the hands-on approach and supervision were left to paid staff. In my capacity as voluntary Chairman I was a figure head visiting on average twice a week for short periods and got caught up in this saga although that should not have been the case. Being the Chairman I had to take the brunt of the responsibility along with the other board members. This entire episode is a part of my life that I recall with much devastation and horror as considering all that I have stood for over many years I would not in a million years have thought this would ever have happened to me.

It was very interesting that for approximately two years after the conclusion of the Tribunal Hearing which was reported extensively by the media because of my profile and being the recipient of a national award at the time, they no longer showed any interest in what I was doing on the activist front. Sections of the media treated me with disdain and short shrift after that Tribunal Hearing, as having spent so much of my time challenging racism and other forms of injustice they now viewed me like a pariah because of the allegations of sexism and racism levelled at me. This just reinforced how much the media can build one up and in the next breath tear one down and destroy ones' good reputation. Considering at one stage a local newspaper journalist referred to me as 'Mr. Race', a newspaper journalist from *The Voice* once described me as the most outspoken black person in Britain, along with the national media who would regularly seek my views on racial injustice and racial intolerance; this was now a complete turnaround that I had to deal with.

In addition there were other external forces of individuals and organisations plotting against me because they considered I had become too 'big for my boots' whilst fighting the struggles and the injustices that I stood firmly for. However with my steadfast Christian faith the song 'I must have the Saviour with me as I dare not walk alone' was my mantra along with prayer.

Jamaican proverb: *'If people nuh like yu dem give yu basket fi carry wata'*.

Meaning: If people do not like you they will make your life and circumstances as hard and uncomfortable.

Chapter 8
My first trip back to Jamaica

'Do not be anxious about anything, but in every situation, by prayer and petition, with thanksgiving present your requests to God'. Phillipians 4 verse 6.

Having been away from Jamaica for seventeen years I was really looking forward to this trip as unlike the one to England by ship lasting over three weeks at sea on the SS Begona, I boarded an Air Jamaica direct flight from London Heathrow Airport which lasted for about ten hours. What a difference this made and it was such a pleasure to touch down in my homeland and feel the warmth of the tropical sun. I had such an exhilarating feeling of being there and since then have made numerous trips with my wife and family to reconnect with other family members. The hospitality, ambiance, vibrancy, hot climate, fresh fruits and of course the beautiful beaches with the warm and inviting Caribbean sea make Jamaica one of the top visitor destinations on ones list and I firmly recommend that one should experience what the beautiful island has to offer.

I arrived in Kingston at Palisadoes Airport in 1977 which was the year of the Queen's silver jubilee celebrations. It has since been renamed Norman Manley International Airport after one of Jamaica's national heroes and its first Premier. My arrival was three days before my wife joined me and I stayed in Barbican, upper St Andrew with my older sister affectionately called Miss D who I was meeting for the first time. It was a joy to meet this sister, her partner affectionately known as 'Porkchops' along with their five children. It is a Jamaican habit and still applies now to give people pet or nicknames and I have only ever known my brother-in-law by the name of 'Porkchops'. He made me welcome and asked whether I drank and smoked. My response to both questions was 'Yes'.

Whilst relaxing in the comfort of their home watching television I was amazed to see a black woman on the screen teaching electronics in an educational programme. I also watched an interesting documentary about the 1975 Angolan civil war featuring the black struggles between two warring sides namely The People's Movement for the Liberation of Angola (MPLA) and the National Union for the Total Independence of Angola (UNITA).

'Porkchops' returned from the shop with a few bottles of ice cold Red Stripe beer which is one of the most famous beers worldwide, brewed in Kingston at the Desnoes and Geddes distillery. He placed in front of me some 'weed' known commonly as ganja or marijuana and being a smoker then, I took out a packet of Rizla, which is cigarette paper and attempted to roll a 'spliff' or cannabis cigarette. He observed what I was doing, suggested I put it aside and made one for me using brown paper without including any of the cigarette material in it. So this was the 'Real McKoy' that I smoked and after inhaling it about four times I just sat dazed and stared in space as if in a trance, prompting him to ask if I was alright. After that I did not remember a single thing that had happened until I woke up several hours later.

One of the main reasons for this trip to the land of our birth was to meet my mother-in-law for the first time where she resided in the district of Wedge Well in the parish of Clarendon. She was reputed to be a formidable and well respected woman who owned a lot of land and was known for being a competent horse rider. I had an open mind about meeting her having heard so much about her from my wife but was still somewhat apprehensive. Finally the day came when we met each other at her home and she made me feel welcome. In order for us to become more acquainted she poured a large drink of brandy for me and one for herself. My wife has always been teetotal so never partook of the alcohol we were about to consume. The brandy helped to relax the atmosphere and release the inhibitions as we spoke freely about family ties and family bonds and the geography of the island. She soon realised that my mother's family in particularly the mention of my grandfather James Mills of Pennington were people who were held in high esteem and came from the neighbouring parish of St. Catherine. The mention of the name Mills seemed to have put her totally at ease and she became more accepting and accommodating of me from then on as her son-in-law.

Jamaica is known for its hot climate all year round and in an effort to create a good impression on my mother-in-law I constantly wore a three piece suit. I was so hot that I sweated profusely but wanted to leave a lasting impression on her not just by way of my personality but my attire as well. I kept wondering why everyone in the public domain was staring at me and later realised how much attention I was drawing to myself sticking out like a sore thumb in my outfit which was not suitable for the heat. This visit coincided with the Jamaica reggae vocal duo Althea and Donna's classic song *Uptown Top Ranking* 1977 hit single which the following year reached number one in The Official UK Top 40 Singles Chart. It had the famous line 'In a mi three piece suit an ting', which aptly summed up my mode of dress.

My wife is the last born child of her parents and was regarded as the pet of the family and the apple of their eye with great expectations placed on her to do well academically which she has done. She achieved a Jamaica scholarship to Stratford High school in Kingston and was the only pupil from Wedge Well district and the surrounding areas that year to accomplish that feat.

One of my aunts affectionately known as Bibsy was a higgler in the famous Coronation Street market in downtown Kingston. I made arrangements with 'Porkchops' and another cousin Gary who was nicknamed 'Nine Fingers' to visit her at the market as that was one of the requests that my mother specifically asked me to accomplish. I had known her before but it was still a joy to meet her again some seventeen years later on this my first trip back to my homeland. 'Nine Fingers' demeanour was such that he never smiled at all, was tall in stature being over six feet in height and had the appearance of someone you would not 'mess with'. I also noticed he hardly said a word and even when people called out to him with a salutation he never acknowledged them with his body language or an audible response. It was only much later that somebody told me that he was dumb and that came as a major surprise to me.

During that first visit to Jamaica a man affectionately known as 'Country' and whom I became friendly with offered me a small 'bag of weed', marijuana to take back to England as a present because he knew that I was a smoker at that time. I had to explain to him that I had to return to England to see my two young children who we had left in the care of my mother and under no circumstances would risk bringing such an illegal substance through customs. He really did not mean any harm and was showing his good natured and kind hearted spirit without realising the serious implications that could have occurred as a consequence of being stopped with an illegal drug on my person at either the departure or arrival airport.

On another visit to Jamaica I had a very interesting and traumatic experience at the home of a man who originated from Haiti. A friend had invited me to this person's home and immediately I became cognizant of the huge number of images of cats that decorated the place. To be quite frank it was rather spooky and reminds me of the *Harry Potter* films and books. As an adult I was never a cat lover and although these were not alive, but just pictures they seemed to freak me out even more. I could not wait to leave the place and to this day I remember that experience as if it was yesterday. For me this episode is worse than the anecdotes and stories one hears about duppies (ghosts) in Jamaica real or unreal, imagined or unimagined. So there developed my phobia of cats and one that I had to try to get rid of.

On returning home to England and looking at trees I often spotted a brown cat amongst them which was rather peculiar. As this kept occurring I became paranoid and concerned. It was suggested that there was a need to confront this irrational fear of cats which I had now clearly developed. So one day whilst in Saltley, Birmingham a friend now deceased nicknamed 'Sticky' told me that God made people to rule over all things including animals and whenever I see a cat I should attack it. With that advice firmly planted in my mind I decided to overcome this morbid fear of cats by being aggressive whenever I saw one.

The final straw happened late one night whilst returning from my sister's house in the Medway, Yardley as I encountered a brown cat near a tree. I ran towards it with a piece of broken fence intending to kill it but it ran and disappeared. Since then my fear of cats has suddenly gone away and the ironic end of this tale is that as a family we now own a domestic ginger cat. It was brought home by my wife having been rescued from impending death as it was one of a litter destined to be put down. My wife who was well aware of my dislike for cats felt so sorry at the time for this lovely kitten which we have named Crystal. He is now aged five and I love him to bits which I never thought was humanly possible.

Jamaican proverb: *'Play stone kill bud'*.
Meaning: One person's fun and games may have serious consequences for another.

Chapter 9
Problems faced by the
African-Caribbean community and solutions

*'For the spirit God gave us does not make us timid, but gives
us power, love and self discipline'.*
—2nd Timothy 1 verse 7

This subject is a complex, sensitive and often misunderstood issue
which we as African-Caribbean people tend not to want to face up to.
It is part of our denial and the problems we need to deal with in order
to progress. I feel it is incumbent on me to address this important issue
and the book would be incomplete without attempting to do so instead
of sweeping it under the carpet. Often one hears people talking about
us as an ethnic group in private discussions but few ever dare to
commit to addressing it openly or in written submissions, etc. It is of
paramount importance that with my wealth of experience over the
many years of struggles, strifes and tribulations campaigning for equal
rights and justice in particular of African-Caribbean people that I am
able to write on this subject matter.

Due to our constant denial, apathy and inertia we tend to get
limited resources, get left behind in the political and economic arena
and end up being marginalised, forgotten or fighting for the few
crumbs and handouts that fall from the Master's table (the powers
that be). Thus allowing others to benefit from this as we do not seize
the time, the opportunity, the initiative or the moment. Constant
bickering, internal wrangling infighting and destructive criticism
amongst us as African-Caribbean people do not help our cause one
iota. What is also of concern is the 'crab in the barrel' syndrome
one often encounters which is pulling down each other just as the
crab tries to escape from the depth of the barrel by climbing on the
backs of others. We sometimes tend to do likewise at other people's
expense and we need to stop doing that.

The 'freeness mentality' which is all about wanting things including goods and services for nothing tends to exist a lot in our community and is yet another area of concern which we need to address as it is off putting, demoralizing and not how anyone running a business venture should operate. The sign often displayed in business places which reads, 'Please do not ask for credit as a refusal often offends' readily springs to mind and I totally subscribe to that view as no one can run a successful business based on constant credit.

Sustainability and having a powerful economic base are certainly areas in which we as an African-Caribbean community have been lacking despite being in Britain for a long time. I often hear people ask the question what have we as a community got to show for ourselves. There is no denying the fact that we have achieved a lot in the fields of education/academia, business, religion, politics, community initiatives, law, science, the performing arts, journalism, music, sports to name but a few but still have a far way to go in terms of true lasting and sustainable equality and justice. Our legacy and footprint are missing from a lot of the achievements and accomplishments in Britain and are often marginalised. As a people we need to make sure that they are recorded for posterity.

One of the major problems encountered was that banks in Britain would find excuses never to give us loans or any form of credit in order for us to establish and develop our economic base on the first rungs of the ladder. Some people from the Caribbean were not able to open bank accounts and relied on the old fashioned tradition of trustworthiness by 'throwing partner or pardner'. This meant one person with integrity known as the 'banker' was entrusted with collecting each month a sum of money from others who had joined the scheme and at the end of the month one person would get a lump sum but no interest. The idea was to encourage people within the scheme to save and was quite effective and it still happens today in Britain. This traditional practice helped individuals to place a monetary deposit on their family home, send for relatives from abroad and maintain relatives overseas as well to name a few of the many benefits derived from it. This clear form of self help against the odds is commendable and has certainly been a success for many involved especially in those early years of trials and tribulations and lack of support from financial institutions such as banks. Without that 'partner/pardner' money a lot of us would not have survived as it was a God send towards our economic development.

Over the many years of seeing our community renting properties especially in the early days I am mindful that many have finally got themselves on the property ladder and are now owner occupiers and that is commendable against the struggles they encountered along the way. However the same cannot be truly said about business enterprises and business ventures in terms of ownership of properties on a large scale and that is rather worrying. Weddings, funeral receptions, Arts and Entertainment and other special social events are lacking in venues that we own and can use at our disposal and therefore we have to depend on others who constantly benefit economically from our lack of adequacy in this regard. This clearly shows a lack of vision on our part and it is something we need to address for future generations so that they can prosper, survive and not be dependent on others.

It needs to be established that the African-Caribbean community contrary to popular belief are not a homogenous group as there are indeed a lot of similarities as well as differences. However we have to try to negotiate those differences and work on the strengths and commonality that bind us together. Unity is strength and 'United we stand, divided we fall' is a well known phrase which we must adopt as our mantra. We know this well but the reality is we don't often practise it and that is to our detriment.

It pains me to see some African-Caribbean people in Britain denying their own cultural heritage and cultural identity at the expense of embracing Eurocentricity in its truest sense by adopting the proverbial saying 'When in Rome do as the Romans do'. That is easier said than done as according to another saying 'If a man does away with his own good traditions he better make sure he knows what he is picking up to replace it with'.

Defining some Caribbean people as being from a 'small island' such as those situated in the Lesser Antilles in the Caribbean Diaspora and as being inferior to others along with the African versus the Caribbean negativity and the stereotypes which were left by the Colonial masters in the West Indies after years of enslavement back in the nineteen century due to colonial and imperial rule is something that has impacted on our thinking and mentality. It brings about an inferiority complex in thinking white people are better than us and some African-Caribbean people have readily adopted this form of internalized racism and in so doing try to please and embrace the structure of white rule and white supremacy. Divide and rule is historical and, just like the days of enslavement in the Caribbean where the house slaves had more status than the field slaves and thought themselves as better, that did not engender each fully to the cause and the struggle for freedom.

The lack of support economically, socially and politically for African-Caribbean projects and initiatives is another area of grave concern as many from our ethnic group would rather support other enterprises instead of their own. That is a sad indictment of our poor judgement, vision and rationale as how are those business ventures expected to survive if we ignore them?

Reactive versus proactive clearly comes in the equation for our ethnic group as we tend so often to want to put up a fight or get involved in the struggles in a reactive way when the horse has bolted and gone through the gate instead of being proactive, thus thinking and planning strategically before problems come to the fore.

At times there tends to be a lack of professionalism and lack of discipline amongst us as a community and these need to be addressed in the open. Failing to do so by pretending the problems do not exist or they exist and we ignore them is not helping our future generations in their efforts to develop and progress in order to combat racism, injustice and inequality. As African-Caribbean people we need to take heed of the biblical quote, Matthew Chapter 7 verse 5, 'First cast out the beam of your own eye; and then shall you see clearly to cast out the speck of your brother's eye' so that we are in a better position to challenge the powers that be. Put another way, cleaning up our own backyard is vitally important as we then stand a much better chance of delivering more practical solutions to the problems we face.

Punctuality is often referred to in a rather negative and stereotypical manner as 'Black Man Time' with events starting later than planned. This is something that I find rather frustrating and annoying as it is unprofessional and irresponsible. I can distinctly remember on my housing management course the tutor once said words to the effect, 'Never make anyone mug your time and if they do always make sure that you get something out of it.'

For us as a people our failure to challenge each others' wrong doings sometimes because of the fear factor, not taking kindly to constructive criticism or being in denial, only increase the need for these concerns to be properly addressed. I often say 'You can never be wrong and be strong' and as a community we need to take responsibility for our actions, meaning if one has done something wrong the person needs to recognize the faults and weaknesses, learn from them instead of remaining belligerent and misguided. The ability to show remorse is a positive step in the right direction so as to move things forward and make progress. It needs to be said that as an ethnic group of African-Caribbean people within the Diaspora with the same phenotype, i.e. (skin colour) we still have different cultures, languages, tradition, heritage and experiences so will not think and act alike as is often the white stereotype perception of us. As a result of our rich, dynamic and diverse culture and heritage there will be times when we have conflict and differences and that is perfectly healthy whenever they occur but how we deal with and resolve them is of paramount importance.

There still remains a slave mentality amongst us as African-Caribbean people and Haile Selassie's address in October 1963 to the United Nations Assembly in New York famously suggested half a century ago, 'Emancipate yourself from mental slavery, none but ourselves can free our mind.' In my opinion these are some of the most powerful words ever spoken which, if adhered, to would take us all to another level. The consciousness and level of awareness by some African-Caribbean people in Britain on issues pertaining to racial discrimination, racial oppression, racial abuse and racial harassment fills me with horror in that they do not have any understanding or clue about the dynamics and the subtleties let alone the blatant forms of racism. It is extremely worrying when I often hear African-Caribbean people profess to have never experienced racism. I really am amazed and wonder what planet are they living on as racism still remains a way of life for many people across the world and Britain is no exception to that fact.

I did not come to a situation whereby I am less ignorant of this pernicious evil racism but have made sure to educate myself mentally, psychologically, religiously and politically over a number of years. I have done so from various sources including historians, key scholars, black icons and history books with CLR James, Harper Lee, Black Jacobins, Walter Rodney, Dr Eric Williams, James Baldwin, Frantz Fanon, Chinua Achebe, Maya Angelou, Toni Morrison and Angela Davis to name but a few having an impact on my life.

That is why it is of paramount importance that the British school curriculum needs to place more emphasis on educating all children, on the numerous and varied accomplishments and achievements over the many years of black people. This needs to include the history prior to the enslavement of black people when our African ancestors were rulers, leaders, kings, queens, merchants, scientists, inventors and architects in their own right. Just as every government that comes to power in Britain insists on all schools being taught the history of the Battle of Hastings and the Norman conquest of 1066, the same should be done about the Black Moors and the conquest of Europe. This is about comparing and contrasting and presenting a more level playing field instead of the one dimensional take on British history done from a rather Eurocentric viewpoint. The African proverb 'Until the story of the hunt is told by the lion, the tale of the hunt will always glorify the hunter' springs to mind as the education syllabus needs to be more rounded in covering all aspects of black history so all children get less of a narrow minded and blinkered approach to what has gone on before.

England has been well known over the centuries for its Christian doctrine with the established denomination being the Church of England or the Anglican Church. The Roman Catholic Church also has a wide following. However over the past few decades a number of black led churches have come to prominence and are now well established across the country. These black majority churches came about partly because of the racism directed at black people in predominantly white Christian churches which were not at all welcoming to them as immigrants on their arrival and beyond.

For many years the name for this group of churches was Council of Black Led Churches until it changed recently to Council of Black Majority Churches. Countless stories and experiences of being refused entry to some of these white led churches which are supposed to be the House of the Lord raised more than a few eyebrows. This blatant form of racism was reflected across the entire country in other areas such as refusal in employment, refusal in social and public housing and refusal of entry to night clubs and other social activities to name but a few. Yet some white people have constantly asked us to forgive them and then continue to do the same thing over and over again. As the Bible says on the subject of forgiveness in Matthew 18 verse 22 the number seventy times seven is mentioned, meaning every time one should forgive but I have to seriously ask the question, when is enough really enough in this regard? There is a saying 'Once is a mistake, twice is a co-incidence, thrice is a pattern' and that is another way of looking at it.

The black churches on the whole have filled the enormous gap of making sure that people who want to express, embrace and celebrate their Christian faith in a safe environment can do so without feeling ostracized, marginalized and being on the receiving end of racism. However some of the black churches seem to lack structure and vision in terms of leadership as well as a sense of unity. Getting their hands dirty championing the struggles and issues faced by the black community seem to be outside of their comfort zone and that is of great concern. Some have developed what I would describe as a 'fear mentality' and stay quiet and far away from anything that they deem to be of a political nature. When black people feel constantly under attack by the police and the system at large they conveniently turn a blind eye and leave it to activists such as myself to deal with the struggles. Religion and politics are intertwined, inseparable and a way of life and the churches cannot take the approach of not wanting to engage in the fight for social justice.

Some of these church organizations seem to be of the firm belief that God will drop Manna from heaven instead of helping themselves and others to achieve their goals and aspirations. I am of the opinion that action alongside faith and prayers go hand in hand. One is not at the expense of the other and what is needed is more proactive involvement of the church and its leadership in order to effectively address and change the issues affecting the black community.

Unlike the American experience of Rev. Dr. Martin Luther King, an ordained Baptist Minister at the forefront of the Civil Rights Movement with the Civil Rights Acts of 1957, 1960 and 1964 heralding and bringing about major changes for the lives and welfare of black people, the experience in England in these black majority churches is the complete opposite and a cause for concern. America is still struggling with how it treats black people but Britain is lagging way behind. What a difference it would make if all the black church leaders such as pastors, deacons and bishops were to collectively come together and champion the everyday causes and struggles of the black community and be more proactive in their approach to blatant racism. It would send out the most powerful message to society at large and I strongly recommend this as one of the ways forward.

The black youths of today keep using the blame culture by saying that the older generation has not done enough to make life better for them and I constantly have to disagree with that often heard sentiment. My generation and that of my parents fought assiduously with the tools and weapons at their disposal and achieved a great deal given the multiplicity of facets including inequality and injustice that they still faced socially, economically and politically.

Black youths are constantly labeled in a negative way and often end up being overrepresented from an early age in local authority care being placed in special needs groups in the education system with vast numbers being excluded from school. High unemployment, high drop-out rates at the tertiary level, constant police harassment and brutality, regular and unwarranted police stop and search along with larger numbers of incarceration in the Criminal Justice System contribute to further stigmatization. Increased detention under the Mental Health Act, deaths in custody, longer prison sentences instead of Community Orders along with homelessness all add to the real growing sense of frustration, fragmentation, estrangement and alienation faced by them. To a certain extent, having been part and parcel of this drive for equality and justice for so long I can empathize and fully understand the sense of despair, frustration and anger that black youths have to contend with on a regular basis. It can be demoralizing, heartbreaking and soul destroying to witness the constant oppression and marginalization of a group based on their skin colour.

However there is a degree of lack of respect by some black youths towards their elders which is not acceptable and needs to be addressed within our community. It is hardly surprising some adopt such a negative stance as I am acutely aware from encounters where sometimes other African-Caribbean people make subtle and indirect references to the older generation which can be deemed as ageist. That is not a good approach to adopt and people who do that need to change to a far healthier mindset.

I am in favour of positive and effective mentoring and shadowing schemes so that the baton of experience is not dropped like in a relay race but passed into a safe pair of hands. No one should want to hang on to roles indefinitely as none of us are indispensible but others need to step up to the mark instead of aiming negative criticisms at those who have fought the battle for many years which they have benefitted from.

We have managed to educate a lot of our black children who have established themselves as high achievers in their chosen career fields. Having said that every generation makes mistakes and is inclined to blame the previous one for their failings and shortcomings. However given our history, our lived experience, our lived reality and against the odds we have managed to overcome many of the hurdles, barriers and obstacles placed in our way. We must not be complacent: we must notice and inspire the next generation to continue in their efforts to achieve success as we the older generation pass on the relay baton with sound advice and words of wisdom.

There is a school of thought where some people argue that black people like to use the 'race card' at every opportunity and are always claiming racism. I refute any notion pertaining to this widely held belief and would argue that we do not use it as often as we should even though we are clearly entitled to do so. The question one should ask in the first instance is why are there statutes and laws making racism illegal and unlawful? My view is that Britain is a society that remains racist to the core hence the need for meaningful legislation to remedy the situation. The 50 year old Race Relations Act has been subjected to various changes since its existence and in its place is the 2010 Equality Act which, if used to its full extent and effectively, would help to stem the systematic tide of endemic racism that black people have to endure on a daily basis.

In Britain as African-Caribbean people we are often accused of having a 'chip on our shoulder' in that we are sensitive and get easily upset when faced with the white Eurocentric humour which is often derogatory and racist. We are expected to just grin and bear it. I do not have any 'chip on my shoulder' as my cultural community means that I have ground provisions such as yam, green banana, sweet potato, plantain, dasheen, breadfruit, to name but a few on my shoulder. The Jamaican proverb interpreted to mean 'What is joke to you is death to me' bears home this valid point and one needs to be mindful of that including other people's feelings.

One of the major problems that we as African-Caribbean people face is the culture of fear and fear factor of British society and how we are perceived by the Establishment. It is a coward legacy that makes us even afraid to document our history, our struggles and our life stories of which we should all be proud of and willing to share with others, especially the future generations to enrich and empower them in terms of their very existence and being. One of the aims of this book is to try and break that cycle of not being proud of our history, culture and heritage and who we are as a people. That should bring about a willingness to share our history in print for others to read, digest and benefit from.

I am rather frustrated and disappointed on witnessing some African-Caribbean people who are not prepared to put their head above the parapet and take a stand on important issues pertaining to equality and justice. Having done this so often without the fear factor and making many sacrifices in the process, I remain concerned about how a lot of black professionals conveniently bury their head in the sand instead of being assertive to challenge the status quo for fear of likely repercussions. As a result this warped mentality reinforces and perpetuates the mindset and social conditioning that we have almost accepted without questioning even to the extent of not being able to document our lived experiences.

Although some historians and academics regard the Willie Lynch syndrome as a hoax, which was an address purportedly delivered by him to an audience on the bank of the James River, Virginia in 1712 regarding control of slaves within the colony, it still strikes a chord with me of how some black people tend to operate. The verbatim account of a short speech given by him as a slave owner in which he tells other slave masters that he has discovered the "secret" to controlling black slaves by setting them against one another is similar to how some black people to this day behave in an effort to please the Establishment in Britain. A classic example of that is some light skinned people feel that they are superior to people of a darker skin colour.

Jamaican proverb: *'Rain a fall but dutty tough'*.
Meaning: Income is coming but not enough to meet all needs.

Chapter 10
Conflict with my sister
leading up to the death of our mother

'He said, Hearken, all Judah, you inhabitants of Jerusalem, and you King Jehoshaphat. The Lord says this to you: Be not afraid or dismayed at this great multitude; for the battle is not yours, but God's'.
—2nd Chronicles 20 verse 15.

People often talk about sibling rivalry and being the older of my mother's two children she took me everywhere and left my younger sister behind with relatives. This did not go down well as she would end up crying which is understandable for any child in that situation, even though our mother meant no harm by doing that as she made sure to leave her in the protective custody of other trusted family members. However to this day my sister appears to have carried a burden on her shoulders of me being given preferential treatment and my mother's favourite. That resentment that she showed towards me as my younger sister did not come to the fore until later in life when we as a family were living in England and this took me by surprise. Over a period of time I began to sense that she would take a completely opposing stance on any suggestions that we as a family were discussing and any opportunity to belittle me was plain for me and other family members to see.

Because I had no ill feelings towards her I initially was unaware of how much she despised me and to this day I am none the wiser as to what I have done to deserve such hostility. We had disagreements which are customary in most families but ended up reaching compromises with our mother's advice and intervention being that we must always try to live in peace and harmony. With that sensible approach we always managed to resolve our differences in an amicable fashion. Our dear mother used to say whatever she had belonged to both of us. My mother's last Will and Testament was supposed to reflect that wish of hers but until now my sister, despite my repeated attempts to discuss its contents has chosen to ignore me. I would dearly have loved even one of my mother's several walking sticks as a keepsake to remember her by and that request has not been granted.

My mother, who died at the age of 89 in 2014 three weeks shy of her 90th birthday, over the years began to have failing health which necessitated domiciliary services visiting her frequently in her home, as her sight and mobility deteriorated. My sister was appointed as the main carer of our mother as she lived literally a mile away from her home in comparison to me living approximately 15 miles away. I regularly visited my mother and gained access with keys that she had given to me. It was becoming rather difficult for our ailing mother to maintain her independence and the decision was made for her to live with my sister permanently because her house was equipped from arrangements previously made if she was unable to cope on her own.

During this period my mother was developing the symptoms of dementia and this made it harder for my sister to manage looking after her alongside her part-time work commitments, although she received some additional help and support from the Social Services department. It was rather sad in many ways that immediately opposite my sister's home lived her daughter and our mother's two great granddaughters aged at the time 15 and 18 and being so close by I had expected them to be more hands-on in assisting with her care. Unfortunately this did not appear to be the case.

Moving from one property to another is regarded as one of the most stressful situations that anyone has to deal with, so I could just imagine how upsetting it would have been for my mother, who had lived in her home for over twenty years. At least in her own home, even though blind, she would have been familiar with her surroundings, the layout and have access to her telephone. Suddenly with the upheaval she was now deprived of all her usual creature comforts and became totally dependent on others for her every day needs and existence. Dementia is one of the worse illnesses to be inflicted on a human being as the loss of memory and other consequences are devastating blows to the person experiencing it as well as the impact on the family members.

Conflict with my sister leading up to the death of our mother

Whilst in her new surroundings my mother granted me a last wish before she died, as on one of my visits she asked me to get ingredients from a shop in order to make her famous 'Duckunoo' or 'Blue Drawers' that she regularly gave to me whilst growing up. Bearing in mind that she was visually impaired I grated the sweet potato using a grater which left cuts and bruises on my right thumb. This domestic chore was something that I had not done for many years since my childhood and she insisted on stirring the mixing bowl with a long wooden spoon just as she did back in those early days. When the lovely homemade delicacies were ready I queried whether she wanted her share and her reply was 'It is not for me, it is for you'. That was one of the most touching moments we shared and on asking her why, her response was that she knew how much I loved them. I am utterly convinced that my dear mother knew her time on this earth was coming to an end and it was her way of bringing closure and rewarding me one of my favourite childhood treats that I had not eaten in several years.

I offered some practical and well meaning advice to my sister since she was struggling to cope with our mother by suggesting that she be placed in a residential care home. She really found that suggestion objectionable and that created ill feeling between us which to this day has not been healed. She then demanded that I needed to make appointments to come and visit my mother and I took umbrage to such an unreasonable idea. On one occasion my sister had the audacity to slam the door in my face when I turned up unannounced during the day to visit my sick mother as any caring son would do. She was holding me and other family members to ransom considering the very special bond and close relationship that I have always had with my mother. It truly pained me to be in a situation where I was now being denied access to my sick mother for several months and it caused me considerable stress.

I turned to the police for help who claimed it was a civil matter and they could not get involved as nothing of a criminal nature had occurred. I also sought advice from Birmingham Social Services and they were utterly useless. At one stage, when my mother was taken in to respite care and I was trying desperately to locate her, they knew her whereabouts but refused to divulge any information stating that my sister was the main carer and is the only person they could disclose what they considered to be confidential information.

This tore at my heart strings and left me feeling rather distraught and helpless.

I even went down the route of seeking pastoral intervention from Pastor Ebo, my mother's church priest, who is now deceased and he facilitated two meetings with my sister hoping to resolve this family conflict but all to no avail. Every barrier, obstacle and hurdle was placed in my way by my sister to thwart any attempts of seeing my mother and that was truly painful and remains so to this day. Eventually I had no alternative but to seek legal advice, knowing that my mother could die any moment and ended up in the Birmingham County Court, having applied for an injunction which is a Court Order to allow me access to her. The High Court Judge, in the presence of my sister, her daughter, my wife and I, along with a few other supporters and my ailing mother in a wheelchair made a Court Order which instructed her to make sure that I was granted access to my mother on a fortnightly basis and that I was to be informed if her health deteriorated. The Court Order was granted just a few days before the pilgrimage that my wife and I along with others from neighbouring churches made to Israel, the Holy Land. I was worried that perhaps she would have died whilst I was abroad for seven days, having not seen her for several months up to that point but thankfully I was able to see her immediately on my return.

My mother has always wanted me to be baptized since we were raised firmly in the Christian faith and that wish was fulfilled whilst in Israel a month prior to her death in December of that year. I was able to return to England beaming from ear to ear and shared the good news of my baptism with her. Being blind my mother could not see how elated I was but felt the joy in my words and emotion as I related to her what the good Lord had done for me. She was by then not strong health wise and said in a firm voice 'You must live the life of a Christian'. I am so glad that I was able to do this and share it with my mother before her death. When I reflect on what happened, it is as though my dear mother was waiting for me to accomplish this important deed before breathing her last breath. The pilgrimage to Israel from Cannon Street Memorial Baptist Church in Handsworth led by Pastor Bryan Scott was organised in conjunction with other churches.

I have held firmly to my Christian belief from an early age and always try to practise it in my daily life. It was only just a matter of time for me to be baptised in the name of Jesus Christ. I am not in any way claiming to be the Messiah but when we came across the River Jordan on the pilgrimage and thinking of how John The Baptist baptised Jesus Christ at the age of 30, I suddenly thought this would be the perfect moment and opportunity to make my commitment to my Lord and Saviour a permanent feature of my life. So along with five others from the group I did what I felt was the right and proper thing. To have both Pastor Bryan Scott the minister at the church where I have worshipped with my wife for many years, alongside Pastor Owen Uriah of the Perry Beeches Baptist church jointly baptise me in the River Jordan in November 2014 is an experience that I will never forget.

It was surreal to visit, along with my wife, Bethlehem in Palestine, Jerusalem, Nazareth, Mount of Olives, the road to Jericho, the Dead Sea, Solomon's Kingdom, King Herod's Kingdom, The Wailing Wall and the Garden of Gethsemane to name but a few of the many places that I have read about in the Holy Bible from my childhood days and still do. It was such an overwhelming, powerful and moving experience. To walk a part of the route where Jesus Christ the son of God carried His own cross to Calvary to be crucified to save us from our sins is a moment that I will treasure and will remain with me forever. This spiritual pilgrimage to the Holy Land is one I would recommend to all Christians as it impacted on me in a huge way and should be one of their top priorities.

I only managed to take my mother out once after the granting of the Court Order as she was admitted to Heartlands Hospital, Birmingham but my sister made sure to follow that Order by alerting me to the fact that my mother had been hospitalized. Thankfully I was able to visit her in hospital on a daily basis and was the last family member with my wife to see her alive. Her final words to me were that she could not understand why she had suffered so much having done no wrong to anyone. She mentioned seeing a rainbow and other images coming towards her, adding that because of where I was sitting they could not reach her but would do so as soon as I left. My mother died later that same day, and for those who are not familiar with 'travelling' it would appear to be clear signs of her departing from this world. I sometimes think that, had I remained at her bedside, I would have been able to continue protecting her, which is not to say that her death would have been prevented as when ones' time on this earth is at an end there is nothing one can do to prevent it since death is inevitable.

Following the death of my dear mother and in the midst of planning her funeral, most of which was adhering to her requests and wishes about how she wanted to be remembered, I along with Uncle Henry visited the funeral home where her body was being kept prior to the funeral service at New Testament Church Of God of Prophecy in Aberdeen Street, Winson Green, Birmingham.

In all of my life I have never experienced a sadder moment than when I was on my own with my mother's body for the final time and planted a kiss on her mouth. All sorts of emotions were running through my mind. It is extremely hard to describe the impact and the effect this had and continues leave. I was so weak mentally, spiritually and physically and each time I moved away from the coffin had to return until Uncle Henry finally came in the room saw me weeping uncontrollably and eventually persuaded me to 'let go'. It was one of the most intimate and private moments between mother and son as it really hammered home and dawned on me that I would never be able to see her in the flesh again.

The conflict between my sister, her family and I has been painful, bitter and rather unfortunate in every way. It is certainly not the sort of thing our mother would have wanted for us her two children. The Lord's Prayer speaks with authority of forgiveness and, as a Christian, I truly believe in those words but as a human being it is much harder to forget and erase these painful memories from my mind. I can only keep hoping and praying that we can eventually settle our differences and that time will heal the deep wounds that exist between us. The Lord's Prayer speaks of forgiveness when people trespass against you and I will always do that, including holding out an olive branch in honour of our mother's wishes for us as her two children to both live in peace and harmony.

Jamaican proverb: *'Ants follow fat, fat drown im'*.
Meaning: Excessive greed will hurt you.

Chapter 11
Awards and accomplishments

'And we know that God causes everything to work together for the good of those who love God and are called according to his purpose for them'.
—Romans 8 verse 28.

I value and appreciate education to the maximum level and have always encouraged young people to try and achieve their fullest potential in order to succeed in life. When I recall being told at age 16 that I am too old to become an apprentice that still fills me with horror as I was being denied an opportunity to further develop my educational capabilities. We live in a society which places a heavy emphasis on paper qualifications and to some extent marginalizes practical skills and vocational experience acquired overtime.

Over a number of years black children of West Indian origin were badly let down in Britain by an educational system which deemed most of them to be underachievers, trouble makers and failures. This is demonstrated well in the black historian and former politician Bernard Coard's 1971 book *How the West Indian Child is Made Educationally Subnormal in the British School System: The Scandal of the Black Child in Schools in Britain.*

The Swann Report (1985) entitled *Education for All: Report of the Committee of Enquiry into the Education of Children from Ethnic Minority Groups* fourteen years later also highlighted and reinforced similar arguments. Moreover the eminent black Professor Gus John in his classic book twenty one years later called *Taking a Stand* (2006) further elaborates on the education, race, social action and civil unrest 1980–2005 hammering home how black children have been poorly treated in their quest for education and attainment. It seriously begs the question why, after all these decades, the situation for black children in the British education system remains in such dire need of reform.

With regard to the exclusion of young black males from the education system I was heavily involved for the longest while in tackling and addressing this issue with Birmingham City Council's Education department, councillors and head teachers and had several meetings over the years to engage them in redressing the balance. As a direct result of these meetings I became actively involved in KWAZI, a black voluntary Birmingham based initiative supporting, giving advice, counselling and mentoring to young black students and teachers. I took on a mentoring role at Holte Secondary School, Lozells, Birmingham. I took pride in enabling the school to have a better understanding of the educational and cultural needs of black youths and how to address the problems they were facing.

In 2000, along with other Non Government Organisations (NGOs) from the United Kingdom organised by the 1990 Trust, I attended for the first time the United Nations Committee for the Elimination of all forms of Racial Discrimination (CERD) held in Geneva. On behalf of BRAMU as its Chairman I presented a joint submission to this committee on the topic: The Mass Exclusion of African Caribbean Children from School in Britain. In August 2003 when the next event was held on at the same location in my continuing role as the Chairman of BRAMU, I presented another joint submission regarding Deaths in Custody. CERD, in the periodic conference report, endorsed all the issues raised by the NGO delegates and made recommendations to the British Government to take them on board.

Our two children are the product of a happy relationship and both have been witnesses to some of the traumas, setbacks, struggles and upheavals that I have encountered along the way. They have given me steadfast and wholehearted support for which I admire them a great deal and have of their own accord embraced the education system to their full advantage and ability. I am truly proud of their educational achievements and the career paths that they have chosen. Alongside those negative moments they have seen the positive side, whereby I have received public recognition by way of awards, citations and other achievements regionally and nationally.

I recall giving my first public speech back in the late 1980's whilst working for the homeless project on the topic of social housing and its impact on the black community. This took place at the Federation of Black Housing Organisation conference held at Keele University in the presence of Winnie Mandela, who I was meeting for the first time.

During that same period I was an invited guest to express my views on four consecutive weekly television programmes called *The Nation* presented by Trevor Phillips at BBC Pebble Mill studios in Birmingham on various social and political issues. This was prior to his appointment as the Chair of the Commission for Racial Equality (CRE), the quasi body which was set up to monitor racism in Britain under the Race Relations Act 1965. However due to the (Single Equality Act 2010) the Equality and Human Rights Commission (EHRC) replaced the aforementioned body with all strands of discrimination i.e. gender, race, disability, religion & belief, sexual orientation and age under one umbrella.

In 1998 BRAMU, the organization that I had been involved with since its inception in 1989, was nominated for a human rights award with the Lord Chancellor, Lord Falconer being supportive of it. However the Stephen Lawrence campaign proved to be the worthy and deserving winners. It was an honour and a privilege for BRAMU to have made the shortlist.

Apart from my presence on the international scene I have never forgotten the pertinent issues that impact and affect communities locally and nationally and over the years have been the guest speaker or been on platforms as part of debates to speak about current affairs and the oppression, discrimination and victimization people have experienced.

Further examples of the work that I have done to increase the profile of the issues surrounding injustice, inequality, discrimination, oppression and hate crime are succinctly highlighted here:

Radio interviews: BBC Radio 5; BBC Radio 4; BBC Radio West Midlands; Colourful Radio; London, South African Radio; Free Radio formerly BRMB Radio; Smooth Radio; Heart FM and New Style Radio.

Newspaper interviews: The Voice; Guardian; Birmingham Mail; Birmingham Post; Jamaica Gleaner; Phoenix; New Nation; Asian Times; Jamaica Times; Sandwell Evening Mail; Sunday Mercury; Wolverhampton Express and Star and Caribbean Times.

Television interviews: BBC 1; BBC 2 Newsnight; ITN; Central TV; Channel 4; CNN; BEN TV and Sky TV.

Information about many of my accomplishments and achievements is also available on various social media websites, as I firmly believe that my campaign to enlighten and increase people's knowledge, historical perspective and awareness of social issues is of paramount importance. So with that in mind I have used that medium to maximum effect. You Tube, LinkedIn, Twitter, Facebook, Instagram and Google are websites where people have commented or placed contributions on aspects of campaigns I have been involved in over the years and vice versa.

It is pleasing to see the positive reaction encouraging me to continue the fight and struggle for justice and equality even though and not surprisingly bigotry, sexist and racist language and comments are frequently often displayed as well. I often take pity for the warped minds and ignorance contained in some of the responses and think of how misinformed, misguided and brainwashed their views and opinions are. We live in a fast growing technological age and I would encourage others to use social media to their advantage in disseminating information in order to raise awareness of social issues as it is a powerful tool that does work when done properly.

For awhile I was a voluntary mentor for the West Midlands Probation Service visiting inmates in prisons to offer encouragement in order to get them to change their lives for the better and improve their chances in life during resettlement and rehabilitation in the community.

In 2001 until 2011 I was a board member of the 1990 Trust, a national London based organization that for many years has campaigned for equality and justice on behalf of Black and Minority Ethnic (BAME) communities.

I remain an active supporter and campaigner of Operation Black Vote (OBV) which is tasked with mobilizing the Black and Minority Ethnic community to register and vote in elections. It is a non-partisan organisation established in 1995 and evolved from the 1990 Trust and another organisation called Charter 88. OBV attempts to address the apathy and inertia often experienced in the Black and Minority Ethnic community who due to a multiplicity of reasons shy away from exercising their democratic right to vote whilst others have died for that privilege with South Africa and the United States being prime examples.

As a previous winner of The Community and Diversity Elders Award 2000 presented by the *New Nation* newspaper I regard being in good company since that award has also been given to Nelson Mandela the former President of South Africa who is one of my icons and heroes.

One of my proudest moments was becoming the winner of the Prime Minister's Regional and National Active Community Award 2000 for Building a fair and just community. Initially at Wembley Arena the then Prime Minister Tony Blair read out the nominations in each category without revealing the various winners. Later that same evening during the award ceremony held at the Dome in London, renamed the 02 Arena, whilst my wife and I sat at the same table with John Conteh a former middleweight world boxing champion and Tessa Sanderson a former Olympic javelin champion, I experienced one of the most surreal moments in my life after watching a video of all the nominees. To my complete surprise John Conteh went on stage and opened an envelope announcing me as the winner. Considering the talent and contributions of the other nominees in that category just being in such illustrious company was an honour as I honestly did not think that I stood any chance of being declared the winner. So I was really taken aback for a moment on hearing my name.

Following the unanimous unlawful killing verdict of Alton Manning on the 3rd June 1998, I was invited by Lord Falconer the then Lord Chancellor, to sit on the Home Office Victim Advisory Panel in 2002 for three years to advise government ministers on race issues pertaining to the Criminal Justice System and equality and diversity. The panel members were invited to visit Tony Blair, the Prime Minister at his official residence No. 10 Downing Street, London in April 2004 and following that visit I received a personal thank you letter from him highlighting the contributions that I had achieved in making real improvements in the Criminal Justice System.

Other accomplishments are as follows:

- As Chairman of BRAMU I gave oral and written presentations in 1998 at Birmingham's International Convention Centre to the

Sir William McPherson enquiry panel on behalf of five Black and Minority Ethnic community groups.

• I received the West Midlands Police Authority Community Service Award for significant contribution during the public disorder in August 2011 following the tragic death of three young Asian men in Birmingham.

• As a former member of the West Midlands Police reference group specifically tasked with addressing issues affecting communities, I with other members of that group met the Duke and Duchess of Cambridge during their August 2011 visit to Birmingham following several nights of disturbances and unrest in the city.

• The annual Dr. Martin Luther King tribute held in Birmingham in January to commemorate his birthday which in most American states is a national holiday on the 9th of that month has been addressed by me on five consecutive occasions since 2012. The most recent event was celebrated at Birmingham Town Hall.

• Community Lifetime Achievement Award, February 2013 in Birmingham organised by a community group called Inspiring a Generation.

• European Diversity Campaigner of the Year, Highly Commended Category Award 2013.

• In 2014 I gave a tribute at a Nelson Mandela memorial service at The New Testament Church of God, Birmingham known as The Rock.

• Dr Richard Stone, medical doctor, prominent anti-racist activist and the author of the book *Hidden Stories of the Stephen Lawrence Inquiry* highlighted my work and involvement in the struggles for justice and equality in it. On his nationwide book launch tour in 2014 he invited me to be the keynote speaker in Birmingham.

• Since 2015 I became a member of the Victim Law Forum based at The House of Commons, chaired by Sir Keir Starmer the eminent QC and former Director of Public Prosecution and former Head of the Crown Prosecution Service.

It has always been my desire and dream to visit what I perceive is the Motherland, Africa because that is where my roots originate. So when the opportunity arose I was ecstatic as never thought in my wildest dreams that would have become a reality. In preparation for going having been conditioned over several years to thinking that Africa was such a backward continent I took the precaution believe it or not of buying a torch/flashlight in order to be equipped for trips especially during the dark evenings. I had wrongly fallen in to the trap of accepting the myths and negative stereotypes constantly portrayed by the Western media of Africa being the 'Dark Continent' with a Tarzan jungle type mentality. I certainly had a vastly different experience as the perception and fiction were such a contrast to the reality.

In 2001 in my capacity as Chairman of both BRAMU and Sandwell Racial Harassment unit I attended The World Conference Against Racism, highlighting racial discrimination, xenophobia and other related intolerances which took place in Durban, South Africa from 31st August to the 8th September with over 27,000 delegates. Amongst the guest speakers were Rev. Jesse Jackson, Winnie Mandela, Angela Davis, Fidel Castro and Thabo Mvuyelwa Mbeki the second president of South Africa. The British delegation was led by Baroness Valerie Amos. Along with other delegates I arrived at Cape Town International Airport towards the end of August and was most surprised as to how cold it was because my perception of Africa has always been that it is a hot continent all year round similar to the climate that I am accustomed to in Jamaica. I noticed that the airport was staffed with mainly Asian women which struck me as being a bit strange. That first impression left me perplexed considering I thought there would have been more black Africans of my hue and colour. I took a domestic flight to Durban and recall next morning waking up to the sights and sounds of milky waves due to their whiteness as they crashed on the seashore. Durban to my surprise was a modern and vibrant place with up-to-date amenities and the perception that I had fixed in my mind towards

Africa with the need for a torch/flashlight was quickly diminished. With the benefit of hindsight I realised how foolish I had become being brainwashed, indoctrinated and misinformed as tends to be portrayed by the media.

Quite separately as a community and human rights activist I am known for peaceful marches, demonstrations and protests in Britain and took the opportunity along with my good friend Audrey Adams and Lee Jasper, former race adviser to Ken Livingstone as a former mayor of London, to join Angela Davis another well known political activist on a march in Durban in support of the African National Congress (ANC). Yet another moment which has left a significant mark amongst my precious memories as I remember many years before wearing a *Free Angela Davis* badge as a mark of solidarity when she was being persecuted and imprisoned in her own country, America for her beliefs and ideology. She was one of my heroines and it was without a doubt one of the highlights of my first and only visit to Africa. Chanting songs which I learnt along the way and holding hands with strangers of almost every nationality from across the globe with a sense of comradeship and fellowship sent shivers down my spine and was another of my achievements which stand out in my memory. The songs of struggle and freedom which herald the ending of the Apartheid era were so powerful, uplifting, personal, emotional and heart wrenching and interestingly were not at the time made available to the general public to buy on compact discs (CDs.) These were moments and times which I will always cherish.

It was truly ironic that a day after returning to England from this significant international conference in September 2001 looking at ways to combat all form of racism, racial intolerance and xenophobia the 9/11 atrocities on the Twin Towers in New York and the other hijacked plane that crashed into the Pentagon, Washington, DC took place. So in one breath I was at an event looking at world peace in order for us to live harmoniously and in the next breath people's lives were brought to an abrupt end needlessly and prematurely.

The indefatigable Rev Jesse Jackson whilst on his first national tour of Britain in 2007 called *The Economics of Colour,* in commemoration of the 200th anniversary of the Abolition of the Transatlantic Slave Trade of 1807 organised by Operation Black

Rev. Jesse Jackson in Birmingham with Maxie Hayles shortly after presenting him with the lifetime achievement award.

Vote and the 1990 Trust visited Birmingham. It was with immense pleasure and pride that I was his host in my role as Chairman of the Birmingham Racial Attacks Monitoring Unit (BRAMU) for the duration of the Birmingham leg of the tour. Alongside BRAMU the Birmingham City Council hosted a civic reception in his honour at the International Convention Centre.

I am one of those fortunate to be able to say that I have met this prominent and high profile campaigner on five separate occasions over the years as he too has dedicated his life campaigning for civil rights, equality and justice. To receive from Jesse Jackson a life time achievement award in 2008 for outstanding work defending human rights and race equality whilst on his second visit to Birmingham was a momentous occasion and one that will remain firmly etched in my memory.

I am of the firm opinion that it is only by participating on committees, bodies, community groups, boards and working parties, and political engagement etc that one is able to influence and bring about change. That is what I have been doing for most of my life. It is important to be around the negotiation table as shouting from the sidelines alone is not an effective way to be a catalyst for change. I wholeheartedly believe in being part of the struggle from within as opposed to being on the outside looking in wondering what is happening. Being actively involved is where the real differences and changes take place. However I also accept that there will be instances when lobbying and campaigning from the outside as an activist which I have repeatedly done also bring pressure to bear and exerts influence on important decision making processes.

Jamaican proverb: *'Di hotta di battle, di sweeta di victory'*.
Meaning: Success is more rewarding after hard work and struggle.

Conclusion

I wrote this book as a tribute and dedicate it to my late beloved mother Doris Amanda Lewis so it is only right and befitting that she features at the end. My mother remains constantly in my thoughts and memory and more so on special occasions such as Mother's Day, birthdays, anniversaries, Christmas Day to name but a few. Sometimes on seeing some elderly women it makes me reflect on aspects of my mother's life including her gentle spirit, heart of gold and generosity that she possessed not just to immediate relatives but others who came in contact with her. Her selfless approach was one of her adoring and admirable qualities which I hope has been reflected through some of my work described in this book. She certainly instilled in me a sense of purpose and challenged my drive, energy, passion and enthusiasm in shaping who I am. Throughout her life she always without fail showed her tender loving care to my sister and I and to the end remained a devoted and proud mother, grandmother and great grandmother. I could not have wished for a better mother.

One of my abiding memories of her was during my early childhood going everywhere with her and a particular song that she always sang with the words , "There is a ship in the harbour, loaded with silver and gold and before my wife and children should die, I'll take up my anchor and go. Some say love is a pleasure but I find no pleasure in love, love caused me to weep, love caused me to moan, love caused me to leave my dear home." Even as a grown man I have never forgotten the words of that song that she regularly sang in my presence and deeply regret never asking her for its origin and why she sang it so often to me hence my vivid memory of the words.

The impact of her death has really taken its toll on me and though time is supposed to be a great healer, when you have such a powerful and loving relationship with your mother as I did over such a long period of time, the pain of losing her does not get any easier.

I really hope that common sense will eventually prevail between my sister and I, as that is exactly what my mother would have wanted in terms of us living in unity and peace as a family. Only time will tell as I am a firm believer in forgiving anyone even though it is much harder to forget what has happened especially in the last few months of my mother's life on this earth.

I have really enjoyed revisiting most aspects of my childhood in Jamaica whilst writing my memoirs and from such humble beginnings appreciate how lovely it was. Fun, happiness, mirth and laughter were the order of the day in my early upbringing except for the periods of bullying including my stepfather physically abusing me by dousing me with water whilst I was lying in bed and being abusive to my mother. The good support structures that were in place with my extended family as my mother being the sole bread winner was often elsewhere working to provide for my sister and I did not diminish the loving relationship that we shared.

The solid grounding in the education system from basic school at 5 through to all age school at 15, along with the socialization process prepared me for life in general. As a child growing up I was not wrapped in cotton wool, mollycoddled, or born in the lap of luxury. With such freedom to explore my surroundings, that increased my coping and defence mechanisms which helped in later life, hence my survival instincts kicking in. I was being prepared without consciously knowing it for the fights, battles, trials, tribulations and struggles that I have had to endure with politicians, the education system, police authorities, government departments, bureaucrats, the Courts, some family members and employers.

My so called 'failure' within the British education system resulting in not being able to practise as a qualified social work and thus being denied my livelihood cannot be understated as it changed the course of history and my life forever. A lot of what I have accomplished in life over the many years amounts to social work and beyond as my approach has always been community focussed and not one dimensional. My work as a community and human rights activist locally, nationally and internationally embraces a whole spectrum of issues that have impacted and affected the lives and welfare of many people. Not for a second do I regret any of my involvement in this work and campaign for justice and equality. I will openly and honestly say that although mention has been made of having received many citations, accolades, awards and achievements, at no stage did I set out with that in mind. Those are secondary and not the primary focus of the work I have done over time. It still remains my passion to champion the cause for racial justice and equality and especially for those who do not feel that they have a voice to do so.

I firmly believe that it was a calling from my creator Jesus Christ as part of my Christian faith and upbringing to take on this mantle of helping others. Throughout my life I have always been of the view that there is a spiritual God who if we believe, trust and have faith in Him any issues that we face will be resolved.

There is a sense of pride and joy along with satisfaction in all that I have accomplished and achieved for the betterment of my fellow human beings over these many years. The focus has not been exclusively about black people as it has been much wider since my belief in humanity stretches across diverse communities and colour should never be seen as a barrier to helping others. In an ideal world or Utopia these constant battles and victories would not be necessary but unfortunately the racism and bigotry of narrow minded, ignorant and brainwashed individuals due to their socialisation process and learned behaviour renders it almost impossible to have a society with no forms of discrimination.

Institutional racism backed up by the individual racist attitudes, prejudices and negative stereotypical views and perceptions held by some people in positions of power and control all contributed to me not qualifying as a social worker those many years ago. However with hindsight and their narrow minded views thinking that they have gotten the better of me, I am living proof that with determination, passion and drive one can succeed by overcoming these obstacles, barriers and hurdles even though at the time I felt like a lone voice crying in the wilderness.

My experience as a black man makes me remember with zeal and vigour some of the powerful words of Maya Angelou's famous poem *Still I Rise*:

> You may write me down in history
> With your bitter, twisted lies,
> You may tread me in the very dirt

But still, like dust, I'll rise.
Did you want to see me broken?
Bowed head and lowered eyes?
Shoulders falling down like teardrops.
Weakened by my soulful cries.

I am convinced that my childhood including my mother's discipline and the early socialization process all played a part in conditioning me to fight in order to become the victor in the end.

The deaths in custody that I have alluded to along with the racist murder of Stephen Lawrence who is buried in Jamaica the ancestral home of his parents Doreen and Neville Lawrence were the most difficult sections to write in this book as the pain associated with such untimely deaths is hard to fathom, comprehend or bear. Even my mother's death at the ripe old age of 89, a good innings to use a cricket analogy, was easier for me to expect and write about. My involvement with these high profile cases of the deaths of young black men in their prime leaves me at times feeling numb, hurting inside with anger, sadness and dismay at how their lives and lights have been snuffed out with not a care in the world.

Bullying of one sort or another whether subtle or blatant has featured regularly during my life and I have had to develop coping mechanisms and strategies to deal with it. It has not been easy at times but in the final analysis I have never given in to bullying tactics used by others trying to subdue me whether it is individuals or institutions. Some had a racist agenda to keep me in my place. The simple message I wish to relay is always confront, stand up and challenge bullying wherever it raises its ugly head and support others who are also on the receiving end. That is precisely why I have over the many years fought and championed the rights for justice and equality and will not allow others to trample or intimidate those who are less inclined to speak out and defend themselves.

The white feminists who tried to take me off course in denying me the opportunity and right to become a qualified social worker have ended up increasing my resolve and desire to both succeed and champion the cause of humanity. Their actions have spurred me on to achieve and accomplish so much more in my lifetime and in essence by trying to oppress me it has backfired. I believe that there is so much truth in the saying initially attributed to the biblical account of Joseph and his position in Egyptian society, Genesis 39 v 2-39 that one can't keep a good man down as I try in every way possible to be that good man in my life as a Christian and God fearing person.

Britain voted on the 23rd June 2016 by a narrow margin to leave the European Union. The final figures were 16,141,242 = 48.1% voting to remain and 17,410,742 = 51.9% voting to leave. The leave campaign organisers seemed to take great delight in misinforming the public by using scare mongering tactics on issues such as immigration and sovereignty, stating that they wanted their country back, from whom or what I do not know. Xenophobia and racism were constantly at the fore throughout the campaign and it was truly alarming to hear the views being expressed by sections of the media and senior politicians frightening the life out of anyone who in some instances were from Eastern European countries residing in Britain. They too were on the receiving end of vitriolic racist abuse. There was also a number of black and minority ethnic people who were vociferous in their views of wanting Britain to leave the EU and considering that most were either immigrants or descendants of immigrants their stance on this serious issue was rather baffling and disappointing.

Since the EU referendum result the police have reported a large increase of vitriolic racial attacks and abuse on individuals and on properties such as mosques, temples and some business places. As a remain campaigner the decision to leave the European Union was misguided and divisive as all the European legislation that protected black and minority ethnic communities will no longer be able to do so. It would have been far better to keep the European community working together despite all the flaws, faults and weaknesses. The strengths and positives far outnumbered them and it would have been ideal to negotiate internally instead of the unknown future that now lies ahead. It is indeed a retrograde step and will I fear cost Britain dearly in the long run

It would be remiss of me not to make reference in the conclusion to the police with regards to moving things forward as they feature prominently in my memoirs in both a positive and a negative way. Sadly the negatives far outweigh the positives and that needs to change as some police officers must without a doubt take on board better police community relationships especially in reference to black and minority ethnic communities. Several government backed public inquiries over many years have highlighted this very point and although I firmly believe that some police forces have made progress, others have made retrograde steps which is unacceptable. It should never be an 'us and them' situation and a more balanced and fair minded approach to policing communities in Britain needs to be adopted. Some sections of the black community are tired and fed up of the rhetoric. A far more positive approach in addressing the at times heavy handed manner in the treatment of black and minority ethnic people must be seriously taken on board. The police are at the cutting edge of law and order in Britain and what lies at the heart of the matter is that the British legal system with all its key components must never be seen to be 'a law unto themselves' or above the law.

Music is a good source of therapy with both religious and secular songs playing a significant part in my life and therefore appearing frequently throughout my memoirs. Until it was pointed out to me recently I never realised how much my love for music impacted so much on aspects of my life. Music is indeed a universal language and it has certainly helped to keep me calm, soothe my weary soul and ease the pain and discomfort that I have at times endured. I recall listening repeatedly in some of the gloomier periods to Bob Marley songs from his various albums which all had an emphasis on survival, struggles and standing up for one's rights. Hymns and gospel music have always played a crucial part in my being and there is nothing more fulfilling and uplifting than hearing such joyful sounds at any given time.

A clear picture has emerged of the numerous struggles in my life along with survival instincts that have kicked in to enable me to overcome these barriers, obstacles and hurdles. Reaffirming my faith in God as a sinner like others has given me the strength and resolve to carry on this rocky road and take the rough with the smooth. On reflection no one is in a position to change the past and the course of history. However one can only hope to learn from it and re-energize in going forward in a positive way.

I wish to end with a couple of verses from the hymn 'My Hope is Built on Nothing Less' by Edward Mote (1797-1874):

My hope is built on nothing less
Than Jesus' blood and righteousness;
I dare not trust the sweetest frame,
But wholly lean on Jesus' name.

When darkness seems to veil His face,
I rest on His unchanging grace;
In every high and stormy gale
My anchor holds within the veil.